An honest, inspiring and powerful read. We wholeheartedly recommend this to every young woman on an adventure following Jesus. Buy it, read it, live it!
Gavin Calver, Director of Mission at the Evangelical Alliance, and Anne Calver, Associate Minister at King's Community Church, Oldbury

I can't shout loudly enough about *Beloved*! Pick it up and digest the words of hope, encouragement and challenge. This is one of those books that you'll want to highlight big chunks of and go back to over and over again!
Meg Cannon, founder of koko (thekokostory.com), a website aiming to encourage and inspire teenage girls

Beloved will change the way you view yourself, your future and your relationship with God. It's easy to read and so full of honest, thought-provoking wisdom. I could not put it down out of hunger to learn more about what it means to be a woman of God, and how to live it out in a practical way. Rachel uncovers a new side to topics I thought I knew. An inspirational and totally transforming read.
Martha Collison, quarter-finalist and youngest ever contestant on The Great British Bake Off, *and Tearfund ambassador against child trafficking*

Love: quite probably the most misunderstood and misused emotion in our culture today. We need to learn that the only way to truly love ourselves is first to know and embrace the love God has for us. It's not radical, but for some it feels impossible. *Beloved* opens up those possibilities.
Fiona McDonald, Director of National Ministries, Scottish Bible Society

D1313141

Reading *Beloved* is like grabbing a coffee with a wise and trusted mentor. The kind of mentor who sees more to you, more to your life and more to your future than you might believe possible. Not the kind of mentor who will pull their punches, but the kind of mentor who tells you the truth, even when it hurts, challenges the parts of you that aren't what they should be, the kind of mentor who will spark life-altering change in you. So grab a coffee, find a quiet space, and see where this mentor will take you.
Sarah Percival, Project Development Worker, Romance Academy

Soaked in Scripture and calling us forward in courage, *Beloved* is a must-read if, like me, you're a girl navigating life with Jesus at your side, but with all the questions, challenges and adventures that come with that. I finished the book with my head held high, my gaze lifted to Jesus, but with a glint in my eye as I was reminded of the fierce, wild, surprising nature of knowing I am beloved and can be love too. *Beloved* will remind you of who God says you are and send you on to live out that fierce and free identity with him.
Miriam Swaffield, student mission leader, Fusion

Rachel – on behalf of the many young women that this book will undoubtedly impact – thank you, thank you for writing it. You pour your own heartfelt learning and wisdom onto its pages. In particular, your Christian teaching on beauty is some of the most helpful and grounded that I have read in a long time.
Lucinda van der Hart, associate editor of Premier Christianity *magazine, a presenter on* Premier Christian Radio *and a mum of two*

BELOVED

BELOVED

be free. be full. be fierce.

RACHEL GARDNER

INTER-VARSITY PRESS
Norton Street, Nottingham NG7 3HR England
Email: ivp@ivpbooks.com
Website: www.ivpbooks.com

The lyrics on page 10 are from 'True Intimacy', copyright © 2011 Thankyou Music/Adm. by Capitol CMG Publishing excl. UK & Europe, adm. by Integrity Music, part of the Davic C Cook family, songs@integritymusic.com.

Some names have been changed in order to protect the privacy of the women whose stories I've shared.

Scripture quotations marked MSG are taken from *The Message*. Copyright © 1993, 1994, 1995, 1996, 2000, 2001, 2002. Used by permission of NavPress Publishing Group.

Scripture quotations marked NIV are taken from the Holy Bible, New International Version® Anglicized, NIV® Copyright © 1979, 1984, 2011 by Biblica, Inc.® Used by permission. All rights reserved worldwide.

Scripture quotations marked NLT are taken from the Holy Bible, New Living Translation, copyright © 1996, 2004, 2007 by Tyndale House Foundation. Used by permission of Tyndale House Publishers, Inc., Carol Stream, Illinois 60188. All rights reserved.

The Scripture quotation marked NCV is taken from the New Century Version®. Copyright © 2005 by Thomas Nelson, Inc. Used by permission. All rights reserved.

The Scripture quotation marked KJV is from the King James Version of the Bible.

First published 2015

British Library Cataloguing in Publication Data
A catalogue record for this book is available from the British Library.

ISBN: 978-1-78359-358-3
Typeset in Great Britain by CRB Associates, Potterhanworth, Lincolnshire
Printed and bound in Great Britain by Ashford Colour Press Ltd, Gosport, Hampshire

Inter-Varsity Press publishes Christian books that are true to the Bible and that communicate the gospel, develop discipleship and strengthen the church for its mission in the world.

Inter-Varsity Press is closely linked with the Universities and Colleges Christian Fellowship, a student movement connecting Christian Unions in universities and colleges throughout Great Britain, and a member movement of the International Fellowship of Evangelical Students. Website: www.uccf.org.uk

CONTENTS

FOR DAISY

My beloved girl.
Love will always find you.

x

We, though, are going to love – love and be loved.
First we were loved, now we love.
He loved us first.
(1 John 4:19 MSG)

True intimacy
Is my desire
To catch Your whispers
To carry Your fire . . .

More than living
More than breathing
You're the reason
My heart's beating . . .

So I'm giving
Freely yielding
You're the reason
My heart's beating[1]

BE LOVED

I spill a drink all down the front of my friend's new dress.

She jumps up, flings her arms out, eyes wide, laughing, and a little furious! You've seen it countless times: that funny lurch we make, too late, to try to avoid the inevitable.

Leaving my teens behind felt like that. I didn't want to stay sweet sixteen forever – I was desperate to grow up and start living – but I imagined that once I hit my twenties, I would somehow be different, a whole new me. With unshakeable certainty instead of crippling self-doubt, and an air of cool mystery instead of my awful self-consciousness.

I wish someone had told me.

Not how to dodge the future, but how to embrace it. All of it: the adventure, the loneliness, the confusion, the recklessness, the yearnings, because it became this creative drive in me to seek, to find, to know.

'God, are you there? Who are you? Who am I? What am I here for? Am I loved?'

If you're familiar with these questions, then this book is for you.

If you know how it feels to be small in a big world, and still want to change it, then this book is for you.

If you've made mistakes or faced things that have at times made you rethink your faith but still cry out to God to use you powerfully and recklessly, then this book is for you.

If you're finding your feet as a woman, still act like a girl (sometimes), and know you need a little encouragement to live out your phenomenal female-ness, then this book is for you.

In some ways it's a sequel.

I wrote *Cherished* because I was keen that the truth of our identity as God's

children would speak louder than the critical, cruel voices telling girls they're unlovely and unlovable.

I've written *Beloved* because the girls who read *Cherished* are older now . . . and wiser!

And with age come those experiences that can be at the same time exciting and daunting: leaving school, starting work, going to university, moving out of home, falling in love, going travelling, getting heartbroken, getting married, following a career, raising a family, building a life, pursuing a dream. In the midst of all of this, you might catch yourself asking age-old questions like: 'who am I?', 'where am I going?' or 'what am I here for?'

Here's Lizzie (twenty):

I feel I am always going through a massive change – it's not always obvious to other people. I used to think, 'When am I going to be settled?' I find that I get drawn to people who also love being on a journey where they are changing and growing all the time. I love seeing my friends getting deeper into their lives. Not being static or becoming stagnant is really important to me.

I have the privilege of travelling and chatting with young women about all sorts of things. Geography, fashion and musical tastes might differ from place to place, but one question nags them all: what next? Sometimes they are anxious about growing up and leaving their teen years behind them. Like Erika: 'Next week I'm going to be nineteen, and then I'm only a year away from being twenty. That's so old!' she wailed.

For some, like twenty-year-old Dani, the labels they picked up in painful years need to be left behind. 'I haven't cut myself for three years,' she said. 'You sound sad about that,' I comment. 'I'm not sad I've stopped cutting myself. But,' she admits, 'sometimes I'd still like to be in hospital where people are watching me, making sure I'm OK. I wore the hospital band on my wrist for months after I was discharged, as confirmation of my fragility. Like, "I'm in pain; you can't judge me." I don't need to cut myself now. I don't have that label any more, but I'm still fragile.'

Others, like nineteen-year-old Hannah, just can't wait to face whatever their future holds. 'I'm about to leave home and get stuck into my new life. It's all ready for me, and I love a good challenge!'

However it's expressed, the desire to become more than they already are burns really brightly for all of these young women, yet it's not without anxiety or self-doubt. Will I match up? Succeed? Find work? Find love? Feel confident? Be OK?

Although asked in lots of different ways, in the end our questions all boil down to this: 'Am I loved?' Somehow, consciously and unconsciously, we know that whatever the answer, it will have the power to change everything.

I'm going to try, time and again, in many varied ways, to root deep in your heart the fact that you're loved by God. For you to be able to pick up a flower, pull off each petal, and every time you do that, to say, 'He loves me, he loves me, he loves me . . .'

Simply loved

This book has been written in stolen moments.

My daughter Daisy arrived one snowy January and turned everything upside down. She clung to me in those first few weeks, needing to know if I could be trusted to care for her. Needing to be fed by a love that would nourish her, strengthen her, stabilize her. That's the thing about love: it's powerful. When you reach out to love someone, or when you reach out to be loved, your whole life changes. In a nutshell, that's everything this book is about. Simply the fact that you are loved.

Were you hoping for something more complicated?

It's funny how the simplest things can often become the most difficult to grasp. That's because we've turned love into a feeling, an opinion, an emotion, that excuses or encourages all sorts of selfish behaviour. We don't always believe it when people say they love us, because love seems to come and go like traffic. When we're loved, we find ourselves inhabiting this space where everything seems possible, but when we're 'un-loved', we find ourselves retreating from the world to nurse our love-inflicted bruises.

But that's not the love we're made to know.

The love you crave is here.

And it keeps on giving and believing and hoping and holding because love, as it is meant to be, is defined by God: 'God is love' (1 John 4:16 NLT).

And God is here.

Loving my daughter has changed me forever. Her life and my life have joined forces. When she's buzzing about something, I'm buzzing too. When I hear a song that I love, and dance round the room, she wiggles along. Do you ever picture your Father God being with you like this? Loving you like this? Imagine it: God's great Spirit, tuned into the moods of your heart, joining

your life to his, throwing his head back and laughing when something lights you up, or being deeply moved when you're in pain.

I hope that reading this book will help you to wake up to God's love in fresh, even unexpected, ways. This is your one wild life. The only way to live it well is to live well in love. The only way to live well in love is to let God love you, and others through you.

It will change everything.

So be free in love, be full of love and be fierce in giving love.[2]

Rachel x

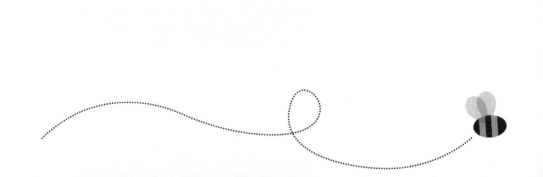

HOW TO READ THIS BOOK

We're going to get to grips with lots of hot topics: beauty, identity, sexuality, relationships, disappointment, regrets, injustice, ambitions, guidance, career, family, future. I'll also be introducing you to women who've been through it all: some of them are doers; others are dreamers. They succeed and fail, lose everything and give it all they've got, stand in defiance and kneel in surrender. They make friends, and sometimes even enemies, but they always love, always hope, always persevere. But when they fail, they always come back to the love that is greater than their own. The secret to their influence and beauty is that they are learning on a daily basis what it means to be loved and be love. I know you will see yourself in them in all sorts of ways.

The Bible and our own Christian heritage is packed full of women who changed the hearts of kings and the outcomes of wars, freed prisoners

and fed the poor, built hope and founded companies, raised children and practised faithfulness, loved recklessly and lived generously. They were both companions to men and leaders of men in bringing God's love to this broken world.

So, in each chapter we're going to be immersing ourselves in a famous or little-known woman's story from the Bible. I want us to let these ancient sisters speak for themselves, and resist the temptation to gloss over the tough bits of their story or glorify them to be who they weren't and aren't. After all, they were flesh and blood like us, self-serving and surrendered revolutionaries in equal measure. But when they choose to pursue Love, they take our breath away!

Eve, Esther, Jephthah's daughter, Ruth, Rahab, Mary the mother of Jesus, the nameless women – at the well, with a jar of oil, caught in adultery, and grabbing hold of Jesus' cloak – all build up a powerful picture, showing us something profound about finding love and living it out with grace and courage even in the most unjust of situations. In their day, men ruled, animals were valued above them, and being a woman meant you were almost powerless to change the world.

Almost . . .

Because against such odds, these women have gone down in history for the

part they played in God's unfolding love story. Jesus even cites some of them among his ancestors.

Wonderland

God's love for you is beyond your understanding.

It can be so hard to get our heads and hearts around the logic-defying, freely given love of God. Even Elihu, one of Job's so-called friends, asks us to

> *Take a long, hard look. See how great [God] is – infinite,*
> *   greater than anything you could ever imagine or figure out!*
> (Job 36:26 MSG)

These long looks can begin with a glimpse where you see things differently, maybe for the first time. I find that the more I glimpse of God, the more I want to see how he sees, and love how he loves. If God is asking us to love other people as we love ourselves, then it stands to reason that we need to learn to love ourselves. One of the best ways to begin loving yourself is to get to know and appreciate yourself.

Wonderland is a collection of questions at the end of each chapter that are designed to help you see God and yourself more clearly as you mull over the ideas and challenges you've just read. You may want to chat them through with a group of friends you can truly be yourself with. Some people find it really helpful to keep a journal.

My sanctuary

For you to be all that you can be, you need to be with God.

He is always loving you, always with you and always wanting to speak to you. **My sanctuary** is a chance for you to find a safe, still place where you can stop and listen to God, free from distraction. If you're not used to silence, this can feel uncomfortable to start with. But persevere. Switch your gadgets off! Silence is a creative way to move thinking forward. You have so much thought traffic rushing round your head, and some thoughts are so big they can almost knock you over. So make time to stop, quieten yourself and think. This will become a precious space where you can be you, just you, with God. Every time you open up your heart to God, he hears you and knows exactly where you're at.

So don't dip out of this bit: good things begin in God's presence.

Your safe place

Your sanctuary could be anywhere: your bedroom, a corner of a room at college, or the local coffee shop. It might also work better for you at a certain time in the day: are you more of a dawn girl or a twilight kind? The most important thing is that you find somewhere you can grab undisturbed alone time. When you find your sanctuary, start each time of reflection with the words: 'Lord, I'm just going to sit here and be the object of your love.'[3] You'll be amazed at what happens as you rest in the loving gaze of God.

Your safe person

Let me encourage you to find someone to talk and pray things through with. Make sure this is someone who loves Jesus and loves praying for you. A good friend of mine once told me that praying for someone is like toasting marshmallows! You don't need to do much, other than pop the marshmallow on the stick and hold the stick over the fire, slowly turning it. The heat does the rest. Find someone who can help you to stay in the presence of Jesus, especially when it feels challenging, uncomfortable or even painful. Knowing that your friend will be with you as you allow God's Spirit to work in your life can help you to linger longer in the place of healing.

> **God sees with utter clarity who we are. He is undeceived as to our warts and wickedness. But when God looks at us that is not all He sees. He also sees who we are intended to be, who we will one day become.**[4]

This is your one brilliant and beautiful life. No matter what has gone before, a blank page lies open before you. Everything is still to play for! So, as you

grab hold of God's love and allow it to seep into your heart, mind and soul, may you find yourself growing in confidence, hope and courage.

Live life with arms wide open. It's yours!

1: BE WHOLE

My ultimate goal is to end up being happy.
Most of the time.
Taylor Swift

Finding happy

Imagine yourself happy.

Really happy.

I like being happy. I like waking up, somehow knowing that today is going to be a 'good' day. Maybe it's the weather, or I've just got a decent amount of sleep, or I don't have much to do. But waking up happy is an amazing feeling. And it's good for us and good for other people too. Have you noticed that when you feel happy, you tend to act 'nicer'? And when you act 'nicer', you tend to look 'nicer'!

All in all, happiness 'works'.

Until it doesn't.

Happiness is elusive, flimsy, passing. It comes and goes like leaves on trees or sales at Topshop! It's a wonderful feeling that we all crave, and we often discover it when we least expect it. We can make other people happy, and sometimes it can be a great motivator, helping us focus on making good decisions, but in the end it isn't everything. Which is a relief, because no matter how hard we work at finding and keeping 'happy', there will be times when it drains away completely as the pressures of life kick in.

I remember meeting Asher at a conference I was speaking at. It had been pouring with rain all week, the loos were constantly blocked and everyone's tents were washed down the hill into a mucky pile at the bottom. It was bad! To make matters worse, I'd pulled no punches about how tough it was to follow Jesus. At some point, I'd encouraged everyone with: 'Being a Christian is a whole lot harder than not being a Christian!'

At the end of the week, I was just getting into my car to head home, when this figure in a fluffy hooded parka came dashing across the sodden field, laughing and apologizing and shouting for me to wait. She caught her breath, and her face changed. It all came pouring out. 'I don't know what to think. You said following Jesus is hard. Why does he make it so hard for me? . . . I'm confused . . . Doesn't God want me to be happy? He does, doesn't he? He wants me to be happy?'

'No,' I said simply.

She gasped. We stood there for a few moments, in silence. Both getting colder and wetter.

Eventually I said, 'Why would God settle with giving you something that doesn't last, when he could create in you an enduring passion for him?'

She was crying freely now. 'But why doesn't God want to make me happy? He's my Father. I've had a really bad few years. Everything's horrible. God wants me to be OK.'

'God wants you to be his. He wants you to be whole.'

'Whole is happy,' she insisted.

'No, whole is his.'

I knew where Asher was coming from. Indeed, she wasn't wrong to want life to be easier. But I didn't want her to walk away from this opportunity to ask God for the best thing he could give, which wasn't happiness.

I wanted her to want to be whole.

I wanted her to want to be his.

Completely. Utterly. Forever. His.

It's easier to ask Jesus to make us happy than to make us whole, because
A. We've already got our list made out of what being happy would entail.
B. We secretly think we could do a better job of making ourselves feel OK than God could.

But the problem with happiness is that it is always only skin deep. If your list is anything like mine, it involves having all the things in life you think you need. But a few moments spent in the company of someone who 'has it all' would quickly tell you that what we ultimately need, we just can't provide for ourselves.

What we need is to be made over. Not simply to be better, but to be new.

Happiness (like a plaster) is a temporary solution to our far greater need – the need for God to remake us: 'Anyone who belongs to Christ has become a new person. The old life is gone; a new life has begun!' (2 Corinthians 5:17 NLT). This is what wholeness is – belonging wholly and completely to God.

Fast forward to the present. As Asher and I chatted and prayed, the Holy Spirit began to reveal to us just how broken she was. It wasn't because she didn't have the stuff she needed to make life easy. It was because there was a war in her heart. It was divided between wanting to serve God and serve herself. For years she had hidden a damaging addiction to sex that made her create a web of lies. It was painful for her to begin to face the reality of her hardness towards God, even as she wanted to love him more.

We got on our knees in the mud by my car. As she poured out all the lies and pain and mess, God took her dead, divided heart and gave her a heart that was free and alive to him, a heart fit for his holy presence. It's what he promises to do when we confess our deep need for him. In the Old Testament he says to the House of Israel, 'I will give you a new heart, and I will put a new spirit in you. I will take out your stony, stubborn heart and give you a tender, responsive heart' (Ezekiel 36:26 NLT).

Before I left Asher, we talked about who could support her as she made the big changes to her life. Then we prayed that her life would begin to be full to bursting with the evidence of God's presence in her heart, making her whole: love, joy, peace, patience, gentleness, kindness, goodness, faithfulness and self-control. It wasn't our list; we nicked it off the apostle Paul, who reeled it off as the fruit of a life that's being made whole by Jesus.

> *But what happens when we live God's way? He brings gifts into our lives, much the same way that fruit appears in an orchard – things like affection for others, exuberance about life, serenity. We develop a willingness to stick with things, a sense of compassion in the heart, and a conviction that a basic holiness permeates things and people. We find ourselves involved in loyal commitments, not needing to force our way in life, able to marshal and direct our energies wisely.*
> (Galatians 5:22–23 MSG)

I called Asher a while later to see how she was doing.

'Terrible!' was her reply.

'Oh no! What's happened?' I asked.

She laughed at the panic in my voice. 'The problem with God giving me a whole new heart is that I feel this incredible passion for getting to know him better. It's changed my whole life. I'm not in charge any more! I don't recognize who I used to be or how I managed for so long to convince myself that I wasn't hurting myself or the people

I loved. I can't see someone suffering and walk by any more. I can't let stuff go that needs to change. I feel more joy and more sadness than ever before. God hasn't just given me a new heart; it's like he's given me his heart!'

Exposed so that we can see just how deep our need for him really is.

Broken so that we can be made whole.

Asher's new life is already bearing fruit.

Grace changes everything

Nothing about us is hidden from God. He shines a light not only on the pain we suffer, but also on the sin, the wrongdoing, we commit that gets in the way of our relationship with him.

Nobody likes talking about sin.

But I love talking about it!

Not in a 'what-have-you-been-up-to-today' kind of way. A real conversation about sin is actually all about grace. It's an 'I'm-a-mess-without-grace' sort of chat. So I love it because I know how much I need God's grace. Left to myself, I'm selfishly ambitious, arrogant, hard towards the people I love. My hunger

for happiness (or simply to feel OK) can sometimes drive me to selfishness where I only care about myself. I know how deep my need for cleaning goes – and I also know that by myself I can only clean up the surface (a bit). Only God can clean the sickness of sin that lives inside me.

The reason why God hates sin in our lives is because it is a bit like a 'Keep-God-out' sign that holds us prisoners to our insecurity and selfishness, and ensures we remain broken. Sin is a strong and cruel slave-master. Have you noticed in your own life that you find yourself returning time and again to the sin you commit as a way of feeling better about the sin you commit? It's a damaging cycle that needs to be broken. No matter how strong we are, on our own we can't break it. We need a saviour for that. The apostle Paul knew this better than anyone did. After years of murdering Christians, he was met by Jesus in a powerful and blinding vision. He got to see the depth of his darkness as well as the even-bigger embrace of grace.

> *What I don't understand about myself is that I decide one way, but then I act another, doing things I absolutely despise. So if I can't be trusted to figure out what is best for myself and then do it, it becomes obvious that God's command is necessary.*
> (Romans 7:15–16 MSG)

Mel asked to meet me to chat. She'd just come back from visiting her friends at university. Their last summer together at church had been amazing. They'd

felt so optimistic about their futures and inspired to live for Jesus. But the parting as some of them had headed off to uni and others like Mel had stayed put and found jobs had been really hard. Mel found herself faced with a loneliness that tapped into all her old insecurities about not being good enough.

She'd had such high hopes for that weekend, but it hadn't gone to plan. They'd argued over the fact that she'd bought another round of shots. Then she'd got separated from them at the club. The drinks were cheap, and the guys were confident. One guy in particular seemed into her. So she ended up going back to his halls.

In the morning Mel gathered her things and took an early train home. She couldn't face her friends. She had to talk it out, so we met. 'I'm lonely,' she said. 'But I'm also reckless – and vengeful. It's like I wanted to sleep with George to get back at the girls for leaving me behind when they went off to university, and for having a go at me for drinking when they're such "perfect" Christians. I almost wanted to be the really bad Christian I think they sometimes think I am.'

Mel is not a bad or a good Christian. (They don't exist, by the way!) Although I wasn't glad about what she'd been through, I was so proud of her for bringing it out into the open, to expose both her pain and her sin. To bring both to Jesus so that she could experience him making her whole.

Paul's wholeness list comes after another list. This time he reels off evidence of a life lived without any reference to God. Every time I read it, I'm reminded that whether we're being promiscuous with our bodies or unkind towards strangers, God calls it 'sin'. And he's serious about it. Very serious.

> *When you follow the desires of your sinful nature, the results are very clear: sexual immorality, impurity, lustful pleasures, idolatry, sorcery, hostility, quarrelling, jealousy, outbursts of anger, selfish ambition, dissension, division, envy, drunkenness, wild parties, and other sins like these. Let me tell you again, as I have before, that anyone living that sort of life will not inherit the Kingdom of God.*
> (Galatians 5:19–21 NLT)

They're all sin because they break God's law and his heart. I don't want sin in my life because I don't want to live in rebellion against the God I love. I don't want to break his heart, hurt other people or hurt myself.

God's law, which Jesus summed up as loving God with everything you are and loving others with everything you have (Matthew 22:37–39), is not a random set of rules that someone came up with years ago to exact power over others with. His laws are a reflection of his character – who he is. He is love; he is faithfulness; he is goodness. Read through Paul's list above again, and ask yourself, 'Does God ever do these things?' You'll find that the answer is always 'no'. Of course, God doesn't have a brutal temper, pursue selfish ambitions or use people, then throw them away. He doesn't because he can't. Not because he is powerless, but because he is holy. He calls us to be holy too – to read a list like this and readily confess our need to be cleaned from the sin that hurts him and us and others.

God longs to forgive your sin, heal your brokenness and set you free to be fruitful beyond your wildest dreams.

Stone woman

The Pharisees (the Jewish religious leaders we read about in the four Gospels) believed that sinful women like her were damaged beyond repair.

The Pharisees believed that men like him were dangerous.

That's why they had lain in wait to catch her 'in the act', so they could use her to expose Jesus. It was perfect: they'd lock her up until morning and then drag her into the crowd surrounding this preacher from Galilee. He'd be bound to feel sorry for her. He might even attempt to forgive her (which is blasphemous, as only God can forgive). Either way, they were convinced that he'd expose himself as a fraud (John 8:1–11).

Morning comes, and the familiar crowd of religious leaders and Pharisees gather in Jerusalem. Jesus is among them. 'Get out of the way! Make room!'

comes the shout, as some henchmen drag the terrified woman into the crowd. Seeing her shaking, people spring back as if touched by fire. 'Disgusting,' an older man mutters. 'Who is she? Vile creature. She smells of the sin she's been charged with.'

One by one, the men shuffle closer, their mutterings of judgment getting louder. Then someone shouts across to Jesus, 'She's a sinner! We caught her in her adulterous act. Moses says we should stone her. What do you say, Jesus? Here she is.'

The crowd of men pull back again, like a wave on the beach. The woman and Jesus are left in the middle, and it goes quiet.

The trap is set. Jesus will lose. The woman will die. Law is law. There's nothing anyone can do.

Then Jesus squats down. It's the Sabbath. He's forbidden to write more than two words on parchment, but no-one said anything about dust. With his finger, he starts to write. At first no-one can make out the words, but even before they read their names and their secret sins exposed to all, they get it. The judgment they want him to mete out on this woman, he's about to mete out on them.

He looks up and shades his eyes from the bright sun. 'If you are free from sin, you cast the first stone. They're over there.'

Then he continues to write.

They walk away, one by one, leaving Jesus alone with the woman. But instead of her being safe, she's now in the most danger she's been in so far, because there is one person without sin who could easily cast the first stone – and he's the man standing in front of her.

'They've gone.'

'Then I don't condemn you. You're free to go. You're free to sin no more.'

He walks away.

It wasn't just the woman who encountered mercy that day. The Pharisees, trapped by their sin of pride and convinced that their judgments on others brought them closer to God, did too. I wonder what this did for them? Did the woman go away and sin no more? Did the Pharisees realize their need for a softening of their hearts towards God?

We don't know.

But maybe we get to complete this story in our own lives. Do you hide your brokenness from others for fear of being judged? Is there sometimes a Pharisee lurking in you who is quick to dish out a harsh judgment on others, even yourself? Do you consider that God owes you a happy life for being a good girl? Have you continued to be in a position of spiritual influence and leadership, even when it's meant hiding a sin that you're struggling with? It might well be because you're afraid of letting people down or don't know who to tell, but all the time you hide behind your mask, you will suffer. Ultimately, any lack of authenticity will haunt you, rob you of fruitfulness and slowly erode your confidence that God could use you.

But if you recognize any of this, you're not alone.

Be whole

So many of us wrestle with the harsh voice of judgment in our heads from time to time. However expressed, it comes from a niggling fear that nothing we do will be any good. We try so hard to control our sin by keeping it hidden or ignoring it. Then, when we find we can't hide or ignore it any more, we fall for the lie that we are broken beyond repair. That all we can hope for is to ask Jesus to help us hold the fragments together.

But there's always hope, because God is always willing to make us whole.

It starts with a one-to-one with Jesus. He alone has the power to condemn us. He alone is the only one without sin who could point the finger or cast the first stone. But he doesn't. Instead, he took all our sin to the cross. He became the one who was condemned so that we could be free: 'In Christ. God put the wrong on him who never did anything wrong, so we could be put right with God' (2 Corinthians 5:21 MSG).

This one-to-one with Jesus might well be painful. There may be times when God will need to deal with our divided heart and break our pride that sets itself up against him. But he doesn't crush us. As uncomfortable as it might well be, if it means being made whole, it's worth it. The grace that saved us in the first place is the grace we need, the grace to keep healing our brokenness. Never think that you're beyond his love and grace. Never think that you're too broken to mend. Bring your brokenness to Jesus. Let him wipe away the tears; let him heal the hurts.

Come broken. Become whole.

Come back to the Old Testament:

> *But he was pierced for our rebellion,*
>   *crushed for our sins.*
> *He was beaten so we could be whole.*
>   *He was whipped so we could be healed.*

All of us, like sheep, have strayed away.
We have left God's paths to follow our own.
*Yet the L*ORD *laid on him*
the sins of us all.
(Isaiah 53:5–6 NLT)

Wonderland

1. Do you have a divided heart?
2. What does it feel like?
3. If you sense God exposing the sin in your life, how are you responding?
4. If you're experiencing 'brokenness', what does it feel like? When do you think you'll be ready to invite Jesus to heal your heart and make you whole?
5. Living in a world damaged by sin can at different times dismantle our sense of being loved and valued, and leave us feeling alone and exposed. Is there anything in your life that you long for God to rebuild?

My sanctuary

The way you express your love for Jesus will depend on the kind of relationship you see yourself having with him. If you know you're broken and can only be made whole by him, your love will flow out of you like a tidal wave. You'll be a reckless worshipper. You won't care what other people think. You'll be too caught up in abandoned devotion.

Having been made whole by Jesus, a woman called Mary defied convention and upset the religious crew with her extravagant worship of the One who made her whole. Read her story below a few times. Pause between each reading and imagine yourself at the scene. Ask God to make ideas and words jump out at you as you read.

One of the Pharisees asked him over for a meal. He went to the Pharisee's house and sat down at the dinner table. Just then a woman of the village, the town harlot, having learned that Jesus was a guest in the home of the Pharisee, came with a bottle of very expensive perfume and stood at his feet, weeping, raining tears on his feet. Letting down her hair, she dried his feet, kissed them, and anointed them with the perfume. When the Pharisee who had invited him saw this, he said to himself, 'If this man was the prophet I thought he was, he would have known what kind of woman this is who is falling all over him.'

Jesus said to him, 'Simon, I have something to tell you.'

'Oh? Tell me.'

'Two men were in debt to a banker. One owed five hundred silver pieces, the other fifty. Neither of them could pay up, and so the banker canceled both debts. Which of the two would be more grateful?'

Simon answered, 'I suppose the one who was forgiven the most.'

'That's right,' said Jesus. Then turning to the woman, but speaking to Simon, he said, 'Do you see this woman? I came to your home; you provided no water for my feet, but she rained tears on my feet and dried

them with her hair. You gave me no greeting, but from the time I arrived she hasn't quit kissing my feet. You provided nothing for freshening up, but she has soothed my feet with perfume. Impressive, isn't it? She was forgiven many, many sins, and so she is very, very grateful. If the forgiveness is minimal, the gratitude is minimal.'

Then he spoke to her: 'I forgive your sins.'

That set the dinner guests talking behind his back: 'Who does he think he is, forgiving sins!'

He ignored them and said to the woman, 'Your faith has saved you. Go in peace.'

(Luke 7:36–50 MSG)

What do you want to do now to express your love and gratitude to Jesus?

Go for it. You're in front of an audience of One!

2: BE FREE

Weight of words

One Christmas I went on a walk with a bunch of friends and found myself chatting with Toni. She was still reeling from something a guy she loved had said to her.

In the heat of an argument he had shouted, 'You're ugly.'

That's ugly!

Somehow, somewhere, this guy had been damaged, and he was passing it on. And he was passing it on to the girlfriend he said he loved.

Trudging through the leaves on our walk together, I was heartbroken for her. She hadn't been physically hit, manipulated or forced into anything. But she

had been wounded. And it had locked deep within her the lie that she's neither lovely nor lovable.

That kind of thing is hard to shake off.

Just like a deflating beach ball retains the imprint of a kick, Toni had retained the shape of this guy's lies. They had knocked her out of shape. It made me wonder if all of us share her experience in some way. Our 'knocks' might not even look very significant to others, but they still leave an imprint, still hold us captive.

Let me tell you something about Toni: she's beautiful. I know you expected me to say that, but she is. Inside and out. She's luminous. She's funny. She is loved by her family and has dreams for her future.

So why did it matter so much what this guy said?

Because what people say can carry a specific kind of weight in our lives that we might drag around with us for years. Like chains round the feet of a convict. Friend, stranger, parent, boyfriend – what people say stays.

We all carry words around with us. In us, on us, over us. Words that are brutal. Words that are beautiful. Words of encouragement. Words of criticism. We pick them up from people, or they are thrown at us. We might let some words settle on us briefly like butterflies: 'You're lovely'; 'I believe in you.' When there's no wind or sudden movement, these butterfly-words sit so lightly on us and feel so good. But then the weather changes, and they're off.

But what if the right kind of words could take hold of us and, instead of trapping us, transform us? What if we could get to the point of hearing the words of fear, insecurity and judgment, but choose not to receive them? What if, instead of fear being etched on our lives, we could be free?

What words hang over your life, or shout out from you without you even having to say them? What ideas frame your life, shaping everything? Even if you've grown up being encouraged to appreciate your tremendous God-given worth, what gets in the way of you believing it for yourself? And what stops you acting as if you believe it about others?

Intrinsically you

I was so glad that when Toni needed it most, she had a day trudging through the snow with people who could push back the lie with the truth, that although people will say cruel things (and none of us can control that), her worth is not something she must gain, but it is already hers and can't ever be taken away. She was reminded that no matter how powerful the 'knocks', she could still reach out and touch the truth. And it switched a light on in her heart.

The truth she discovered is yours too.

This is true not because Toni believes it, or even because it's printed in this book! It is true because it's from God. Anything that is good and true and life bringing is God's. The truth is that the value and worth placed on your life is not of your making or another's breaking. It's intrinsic, in you already, God-created and God-given. This is the truth about your identity that can ultimately combat the lies that try to convince you that you're anything less.

Your heart can stay steadfast – even in the storms of rejection, disappointment or apparent hopelessness.

But you may be coming up against a common problem right now: you're not sure that you believe this truth. In your head you do – it sounds good and familiar to say that you're intrinsically lovely, loved by God and precious in his eyes. But in your heart, you're not convinced. In fact, in your heart you might believe the very opposite: that you're *not* lovely, loved or worthy of love. This is a problem, because no matter how hard you try, you can't believe two conflicting truths.

One has to win out. And for one to win out, the other has to admit defeat and get lost!

Identity wars

I know that when the battle for my identity rages in my heart, I am a woman at war with myself and others. I crave comfort, so I seek out comforting behaviours like shopping, eating fast food, watching endless TV. Comfort-seeking behaviours are varied (habitual masturbation, guy attention, misusing alcohol, hurting our bodies), but they all fail in the same spectacular way.

Because nothing comforts us like God.

Take Amy. Over the years she's had a lot of other people's damage passed on to her, and at times she feels overwhelmed by so much anger. The lies spoken over her have really knocked her, shaping her thoughts. All of this affects how she feels about herself, and influences what she does. Like Toni, she is intrinsically lovely. She has a certain magnetism, and she's a genius in befriending people, but she finds it hard to believe that her life has any intrinsic value or worth at all. She's struggling, but by listening to the truth of her identity as God's daughter, she is allowing a shift in her thoughts that will affect her feelings and actions. It'll take time of course. But it is happening.

In the New Testament, Paul talks about the need we all have to 'put off' old things to allow us to step into freedom. For him, being free is the path to growing in maturity as disciples of Jesus. So he encourages the Colossian Christians to put off their old selves and 'put on your new nature, and be renewed as you learn to know your Creator and become like him' (Colossians 3:10 NLT).

The Greek word for 'putting off' is one that expresses real physical effort, like shifting a heavy sofa or redecorating a house. It requires real effort to change your mind, feelings, ways, actions, future and expectations. But it's necessary, and the great news is that we never have to do this on our own. God never abandons us.

> *Meanwhile, the moment we get tired in the waiting, God's Spirit is right alongside helping us along. If we don't know how or what to pray, it doesn't matter. He does our praying in and for us, making prayer out of our wordless sighs, our aching groans. He knows us far better than we know ourselves . . . and keeps us present before God. That's why we can be so sure that every detail in our lives of love for God is worked into something good.*
> (Romans 8:26–28 MSG)

Put it off

So what are some of the things you would like to 'put off'? See if any of these resonate with you . . .

- You've got so good at accepting the lies people say about you, that you don't know if you will ever be able to believe anything different.
- You just don't know what you're supposed to be doing. People around you seem so sorted, which is making you retreat into your shell.
- You started masturbating because you were curious about your body and sexual feelings, but now you indulge in it so much that you don't think you can stop. The guilt is weighing you down.
- Very few of us are good at receiving compliments, but your current aggressive response to friends' appreciation of you is pushing away the very people you need around you.
- Past failures are making it difficult for you to step out of your comfort zone and give new things a try. People think you're cynical, but you're not. You're just afraid.
- Your love of fashion has become an obsession. People think you're vain, but you're not. You're just insecure.
- When you feel unable to control or cope with something, you find ways to hurt yourself.
- Someone you love is struggling, and you can't fix it for them. It feels like a heavy weight around your neck, and makes you question your ability to love.

If you're in one of these places now, or they are where you sometimes find yourself, remember that Jesus is really good at finding us when we feel lost. And more than that, he's incredibly good at making new and beautiful things

out of lives that feel trapped. He's the Master of new beginnings and fresh hope.

Sometimes we think that new beginnings are all about what *we* can achieve. So often I hear people tell me that they need to get themselves into a 'good place with God' before things can change in their lives. I'm not sure what place that is. In fact, I don't think I've ever got myself into a good place with God. The only place I can be with God is where I am. Where I can hear his voice inviting me to trust that he has good things in his heart for me. That I can be free.

Gone girl

One of my favourite women in the Bible is nameless. Well, she has a name; we just don't get told what it is. Which is probably the point the author is trying to make. Because the fact that she's unmarried, has been connected to many men, and we meet her collecting water from a well at the hottest and quietest point of the day, all says something about who she is – or rather, who she isn't. Life in Palestine for women in the first century was hard.

Around the time when Jesus met this woman at the well, Middle Eastern historians tell us there were about 140 men for every 100 women. Why were there so many more blokes around? Horrifically, unwanted baby girls were often left to die on the roadside for being the wrong sex. This was common

practice in the Roman Empire – it wasn't covered up; it just happened. In Ancient Rome, a father was required to raise any boy born to his wife, but by law he was only required to raise the first-born girl. All other female children were disposable, and often abandoned. In ancient Athens, girls received little or no education. As women were always seen as the property of men, if a woman in Greece or Rome was seduced or raped, the husband was by law required to divorce her – can you believe it? The laws about women were mainly laws about property: who got what.[5]

Why does all this matter? Because, by contrast, Jesus never behaved like this towards women. He didn't use them or treat them like victims. Instead, his treatment of them transformed everything they believed could be theirs, thereby giving them a new identity and a new destiny. And this is exactly what happened for our nameless heroine.

It's lunchtime, and the same as every other day, she creeps out of her house with her bucket to collect water from the communal well. Waiting until midday could almost guarantee that she wouldn't have to see anyone. Seeing others meant being seen. And being seen meant being exposed to ridicule or judgment.

But this is no ordinary day.

And this is no ordinary stranger sitting at the well.

He already senses her inferiority. He already knows she's desperately thirsty, not for the water she's come to collect, but for the life he's come to give her. Listen to how he engages her:

> *Soon a Samaritan woman came to draw water, and Jesus said to her, 'Please give me a drink.' He was alone at the time because his disciples had gone into the village to buy some food.*
>
> *The woman was surprised, for Jews refuse to have anything to do with Samaritans. She said to Jesus, 'You are a Jew, and I am a Samaritan woman. Why are you asking me for a drink?'*
>
> *Jesus replied, 'If you only knew the gift God has for you and who you are speaking to, you would ask me, and I would give you living water.'*
>
> (John 4:7–10 NLT)

To this woman, trapped by the damage of sin, Jesus offers the infinite possibility of being free. And in this place he gives her the opportunity to receive the greatest gift of all: total and everlasting Freedom.

It's the gift that only Jesus can offer. Like water bursting out of the dry ground, it swept this woman off her feet. She leaves her bucket where she dropped it by the well, and runs back into her village, wanting to be seen and heard! No more slinking around, no more hiding in the shadows, no more chains of culture, gender, past hurts and future hopelessness to hold her back. She's met Truth, she's been in the presence of Love, and she's never going to be the same again.

Imagine how much she upset the mores of the day with her new insistence that she could be free!

> *Many of the Samaritans from that village committed themselves to him because of the woman's witness: 'He knew all about the things I did. He knows me inside and out!'*
> (John 4:39 MSG)

What do you think happened the next day?

Eternal life might be bubbling up inside her, but she still needs to collect water from the well! Yet this time it's different. Instead of hiding until the coast is clear, she steps out boldly and takes her place with the crowd of other women heading to the well. A daily reminder to herself and others that there is something and someone who is greater than culture, insecurity, fear, bad choices and other people's damage and discrimination.

I can see her pulling her overflowing bucket out of the well. Water sloshes out. Laughing, she closes her eyes and lifts her face to the sun. No more chains. No more fear. She's free.

So you can be:

> *Each of us is raised into a light-filled world by our Father so that we can see where we're going in our new grace-sovereign country . . . Throw yourselves wholeheartedly and full-time . . . into God's way of doing things . . . You're living in the freedom of God.*
> (Romans 6:5, 13–14 MSG)

Be free

There's no sin prison that God can't free you from. There's no amount of hurt or pain that God can't heal and restore. The only thing I can do is admit that I need him, and surrender all my weapons of attack and defence. Once I do that, I begin to hear him speaking his words of truth over me. Old Testament prophet Zephaniah recorded God as singing over his beloved people when they returned to him. Imagine that: God singing about how happy he is to be your God!

> *Don't be afraid.*
> *Dear Zion,*
> *don't despair.*
> *Your GOD is present among you,*
> *a strong Warrior there to save you.*

Happy to have you back, he'll calm you with his love
*   and delight you with his songs.*
(Zephaniah 3:16–17 MSG)

Wonderland

1. What would you like to hear God speak over you?
2. What steps could you take to let go of the damage and embrace your identity as God's beloved daughter?
3. If any of the damaging cycles I mentioned above relate to you, what could you do to begin to make some changes? Who could you share your struggles with, and who could help you hear God's voice on them, so that you find new ways of dealing with your needs and desires?
4. Is there unconfessed sin in your life that you need to repent of? The woman who met Jesus at the well experienced the freedom that comes from being forgiven and restored by Jesus. Now is a great time to open up the secret areas of your life to God's merciful forgiveness.
5. Sometimes we might wear our inability to accept love as a badge of honour, or an identity that gives us security for a while. But just like all false identities, it will end up causing us more damage in the end. Think about how you already experience God's love, and how you would like to experience God's love.

My sanctuary

Sometimes we keep bringing up our past sins or regrets like scabs that we like to scratch. We might not even be aware that we're doing this, but every time we come to pray, worship or read the Bible, we imagine people judging us for what we know God has already forgiven us for. If you have unrepented-of sin in your life, speak it out to God and confess your need for his forgiveness. He will forgive and restore you. But if you know you're forgiven by God, yet are finding it hard to let go of the past or people's lies, now could be the right time to do something about it.

> **As far as the east is from the west,**
> **so far has he removed our transgressions from us.**
> (Psalm 103:12 NIV)

Draw a picture of yourself (a stick figure will do!) in the centre of a piece of paper, then draw lines out from the figure, like spokes of a wheel. At the end of each line write a label/word/name that you have carried with you at any point in your life.

Go through each one and ask God, 'Is this my name? Is this who I am?' Then be still and wait for God to answer. You may hear his voice, or have a sense of what his response is. As you go through each one, cross them out as a sign that you want to 'put off' these lies, with God's help. It's important to place new names over the old ones to fill the spaces. Here are some of your new names/identity when you follow Jesus:

Blessed
One with Jesus
Loved
Chosen
Holy
Adopted
Free
Forgiven
Cherished
Wise

All praise to God, the Father of our Lord Jesus Christ, who has **blessed us** *with every spiritual blessing in the heavenly realms because* **we are united with Christ.** *Even before he made the world,* **God loved us and chose us** *in Christ to* **be holy** *and without fault in his eyes. God decided in advance to* **adopt us** *into his own* **family** *by bringing us to himself through Jesus Christ. This is what he wanted to do, and it gave him great pleasure. So we praise God for the glorious grace he has poured out on us who belong to his dear Son. He is so rich in kindness and grace that*

he purchased our freedom *with the blood of his Son and* **forgave our sins.** *He has* **showered his kindness on us***, along with all* **wisdom** *and understanding*
(Ephesians 1:3–8 NLT, emphasis mine)

3: BE BRAVE

We are at our most dangerous when we are most loved.
Will van der Hart

You won't believe how much of an issue I have with love.

Is that OK to say in a book that's all about love? (And I'm the author!)

In the past I used to think that the big issues I struggled with were to do with 'something else'. I'd refer to them as my 'stressing-out-about-food' issue, or 'am-I-good-enough?' issue, or 'does-my-bum-look-big-in-this?' issue, or the classic 'me-and-God-aren't-great-right-now' issue. The list went on.

It took me ages to notice that my clever labelling of symptoms got me all distracted from the root cause of my problems.

Love.

 I was hungry for it, and yet confused by it. I couldn't work out why having loving parents and going to a vibrant church didn't remove my deep craving for something more. I found myself pulled in all sorts of directions in an attempt to deal with the aching emptiness I sometimes felt. I was even close to 'de-converting' and giving up on a God who I thought was great for kids, but rubbish for real life.

So what happened?

God found me, all over again.

And I found him.

In my gap year I joined a band who sang a few tuneless numbers in dodgy outfits (it was the 1990s) in towns across Spain and Portugal. I was so hormonal and homesick, I think I fell in love with every guy I met. It was a weird time!

Anyway, to save money, we sofa-surfed in all sorts of places. One night I found myself in a double bed, while the whole family who normally occupied it slept on the floor. It was a humbling and awkward experience. In the morning I approached my hostess to ask if there was a shower. As I had no Portuguese and she had no English, we ended up gesticulating madly. Eventually, she wandered off. I stood in the yard and waited. She came back with a bucket of water and – you've guessed it – poured it over my head!

Maybe that's a teeny bit of an exaggeration!

(In fact, she showed me where the outside hose was.) But that's less dramatic, and anyway, the experience of a freezing cold hose shower in a strange farmyard far from home woke me up spiritually!

What was I doing?

Not in the band (although we were awful). Not even in my decision whether to get a job or go on to further education. It was less about what I was doing and more about who I was being – and who I was prepared to become. A voice deep within me was saying over and over again, 'Sort it out, Rachel, sort it out.'

We got back to the UK, and I headed home with a new steely determination to find myself. My parents have some great woods near their home, so every day for a fortnight I trudged through the mud, head down, jaw set. 'Show me, God, who you are. Show me, God, who I am.'

I'd go to bed at night and write these angry exchanges between me and God.

Nothing happened.

Then, slowly and profoundly, I began to experience the Love I was made to know. The more I raged at the sky, the more God pulled me close and surrounded me with people who knew him well. The more I tried to find my own path to life in all its fullness, the more he stopped me in my tracks and made it impossible for me to ignore him.

And, over time, his love melted my heart towards him, myself and others. And he's not stopped ever since.

I still like to remind myself of my un-loveliness from time to time. I put crazy conditions on God's love: 'He would love me more if . . .'. I look for him doing 'stuff' for me as evidence that he cares. I put damaging limitations on the love I expect people to show me: 'They won't love me if they know what I'm really like.' Or I wait for feelings to tell me I'm somebody worth loving.

But then I'm reminded that I'm only just starting out on this love-quest. What's stretched out before me is a life heading into eternity, where I'll get to see and know more and more of the love that took Jesus to the cross, for you, for me. And, thinking about that, I'm speechless.

When we were utterly helpless, Christ came at just the right time and died for us sinners. Now, most people would not be willing to die for an upright person, though someone might perhaps be willing to die for a person who is especially good. But God showed his great love for us by sending Christ to die for us while we were still sinners.
(Romans 5:6–8 NLT)

Love light

Kayleigh called me. After years of God-dodging, she finally let herself be found by him. She'd been at a church service where the speaker had suggested that anyone who was tired of running away from Jesus should come to the front and sort it out – and she did, with tears and snot streaming down her face. She said 'yes' to Love. She said 'yes' to the One whose love will always find and cover her. And in doing so, she said 'yes' to discovering herself as his beloved.

When did you first find God's love? *Have* you found God's love?

The Bible tells us that we're only able to find God because he has already found us. He's the God who comes looking. Isn't that incredible? He doesn't hang back and wait: he woos us, draws us, melts us with his love. But he doesn't just come looking; he comes to clear every barrier that would prevent us from being loved and being love.

This is real love – not that we loved God, but that he loved us and sent
his Son as a sacrifice to take away our sins.
(1 John 4:10 NLT)

The love we're made to know and show all starts and ends with God. There's never a moment when he doesn't love you. Discovering this is like waking up to a hot day in a wet month, or finding a ring you thought you'd lost. It's like a gorgeous message out of the blue from a guy you really like, or being caught in the rain and then seeing a rainbow. God's love does something to you. Spiritually, emotionally, even physically. His love has the power to change you, to grab hold of you, put you back on your feet and urge you on.

Listen to this description of his love for Israel, his people:

Long ago the LORD said to Israel:
'I have loved you, my people, with an everlasting love.
With unfailing love I have drawn you to myself.'
(Jeremiah 31:3 NLT)

He reassures them of his amazing devotion:

Since you are precious and honoured in my sight,
and because I love you,

> *I will give people in exchange for you,*
> *   nations in exchange for your life.*
> *Do not be afraid, for I am with you;*
> *   I will bring your children from the east*
> *   and gather you from the west.*
> (Isaiah 43:4–5 NIV)

See the dimensions of his love? More than a feeling or someone's opinion or an emotion in a moment, your loved-ness and your loveliness are an indisputable fact. Even in the wildest storm, God's love is your shelter, your safe place, your path home. His love gives and believes and hopes and holds. It wakes you up to the possibilities of all you can become.

We are really loved.

But the reality is, I haven't always lived out of that place of secure, unbreakable loved-ness. Instead, I've often been motivated by my vulnerabilities, my need for approval, affirmation or attention. Living with a sense of a lack of love brings an emotional and spiritual poverty that can leave us feeling we're always afraid.

But we're not designed to live in fear.

Brave

There's a powerful story in the Bible of a woman who for twelve years had experienced vaginal bleeding, making her sick and a social outcast. According to the law of Moses, anyone who touched her would immediately be contaminated. Amazingly, her heart remained steadfast, so when she heard about Jesus healing people, she took her weak body miles just to get close to him. There's a crowd jostling around him. The noise is deafening. She's behind him. She's not allowed to touch anyone. But although she is risking exposure, ridicule, rejection, her desperation is making her brave . . .

And a woman was there who had been subject to bleeding for twelve years. She had suffered a great deal under the care of many doctors and had spent all she had, yet instead of getting better she grew worse. When she heard about Jesus, she came up behind him in the crowd and touched his cloak, because she thought, 'If I just touch his clothes, I will be healed.' Immediately her bleeding stopped and she felt in her body that she was freed from her suffering.

At once Jesus realised that power had gone out from him. He turned round in the crowd and asked, 'Who touched my clothes?'

'You see the people crowding against you,' his disciples answered, 'and yet you can ask, "Who touched me?"'

But Jesus kept looking around to see who had done it. Then the woman, knowing what had happened to her, came and fell at his feet

and, trembling with fear, told him the whole truth. He said to her, 'Daughter, your faith has healed you. Go in peace and be freed from your suffering.'
(Mark 5:25–34 NIV)

He feels something leave him, just as she feels life entering her. He calls her 'daughter', publicly restoring her identity and dignity. It's an immediate transformation. Her boldness becomes an inspiration to others who dare to believe that they too can reach out for his healing.

Wherever he went – in villages, cities, or the countryside – they brought the sick out to the marketplaces. They begged him to let the sick touch at least the fringe of his robe, and all who touched him were healed.
(Mark 6:56 NLT)

Jesus is worth grabbing!

Reach out

God's love is high and wide and deep and strong. It doesn't make sense and it's totally undeserved. You are invited to step out into this incredible love-scape, to have this love sealed in your heart so that your life overflows from it. I meet so many Christians who believe that once they've messed up, they've lost God's love, that somehow they're soiled goods in his eyes.

I remember cradling a friend in my arms as she sobbed over and over again, 'God can't love me now.' We read through Romans 6 and felt the beautiful weight of Paul's words reminding us that in following Jesus, our old selves were nailed to the cross and, with Jesus, we rise to a new life. Our past sin is dead.

A great way to reach out to God is to step out in faith believing that he's there. I find it helpful sometimes to challenge myself to start behaving as if I have nothing to fear and nothing to prove. Ask yourself, 'If I didn't have to prove myself in this situation, what would I do differently?' Make a list of situations recently where you wanted to do something, but you held back because you were afraid of ridicule or judgment. It could be a sin you wanted to confess, but were afraid that it was too great for God's love to cover. Or you may have wanted to share a testimony, speak up for someone at work/college or spread God's love, but you felt afraid.

A prayer:

Lord, I'd love an opportunity to step out of my comfort zone and act in love. I have no doubt that you'll give me one (or more!), so when it comes, please give me courage to step out.

Live out

When you know you're truly loved, you're able to live out of who you really are. You're not loving others out of any need for affirmation and approval, nor are you being hindered or diverted by your needs and inadequacies. When you're doing this, you're capable of really loving and really living. Real love is when you're generous to someone without expecting anything from them in return. When God's love releases you in your real love-capacity, you'll notice those around you who need you to love them like that.

A prayer:

Lord, I long to love others bravely, not out of my inadequacies and needs. Help me to bring those deep fears and insecurities to you. Help me to love bravely and dangerously!

Eschet chayil

There's a woman in the Bible who is one of those 'step-up' girls! She presents a powerful picture of who God desires women to be. Solomon opens his description of her with these famous words: 'Who can find a virtuous woman? for her price is far above rubies' (Proverbs 31:10 KJV).

If you read on, you'll soon discover that she's a bit of a superwoman: expert in domestic and business skills. It's awe-inspiring and (on first reading) a little depressing – is there anything she *can't* do? But when I read it again, what really grabs my attention is not what she does, but who she is. In Hebrew it reads: 'Who can find a[n] *eschet chayil*?'

She's called a woman (*eschet*), using the same word that God uses to describe the creature he has made as a companion to Adam in Genesis, but she's something else as well (*chayil*), and that something else has been translated in a variety of ways: 'virtuous and capable' (NLT), 'good' (MSG) and 'of noble character' (NIV).

Lovely.

But aren't we missing something? Being 'good' and 'capable' are not things to sniff at, but when the word *chayil* appears in the rest of the Bible, it doesn't mean 'good' and 'capable'; it could also mean 'forceful' and 'mighty'. When the angel of the Lord calls Gideon to defend Israel against Midianite oppression, he says, 'Mighty [*chayil*] hero, the LORD is with you!' (Judges 6:12 NLT). The word used to describe God in Habakkuk 3:19, 'God is my strength!', is God is my *chayil*.[6]

Imagine if the way *chayil* is used in other passages could shine some light on how God sees us as women . . . God designed us to be brave women of valour!

If you have the Spirit of God at work in your life, you are *chayil*. You have what it takes to stand strong in the Lord, to stand in the gap for others, to set the tone in your home, university or workplace with your love and faithfulness, not to be afraid to face the past, present or future.

I work with some young women who struggle with anger and aggression. They're often afraid that unless they use violence or force, they won't be heard or respected. To outsiders they look tough, strong, brave. But underneath they're hurt and scared. For years they've suffered at the hands of others who misused their strength and power. Being brave isn't about being loud, or bossy, or manipulative. It's about taking a stand, opening your eyes to others, stepping into the fray – whatever that might be.

Let me tell you about some of the times I've witnessed the *chayil* shining through the women I know:

There are no other Christians at her sixth form, so Anna is praying for opportunities to share her love for Jesus with her new friends, but also finding the courage to speak and live it out.

Tarn is realizing that remaining silent about her 'boyfriend' attacking her is making other girls more likely to be hurt by him in the future, so she's beginning to speak out.

After a few years of being single, Alex is at last dating a Christian guy. Determined not to jump into the wrong decision, she's inviting her close friends to help her seek God for this new relationship.

Rebecca was diagnosed with cancer last year, and the intensive treatment made all her hair fall out. She uses social media to share through vlogs and blogs her story of despair and hope, knowing that her life is in God's hands.

Their bravery shines, doesn't it? As women, we're designed to be brave. So, whatever your story, and however your bravery looks, reach out and begin to discover that you're braver than you think you are!

Wonderland

1. What are some of your vulnerabilities?
2. How do your fears or anxieties hold you back?
3. How do you respond to the idea that God invites you to be brave?
4. What do your acts of bravery look like?
5. When have you been encouraged or inspired by someone's everyday bravery?

My sanctuary

'**I'm loved, yet . . .**' is a recognition of your needs or inadequacies that hold you back. '**I'm loved, so . . .**' is your chance to name your hopes for your life as you step into the wonderful and empowering love of God.

I asked some young women to finish these sentences. Here's what they wrote: pithy but powerful snapshots of what they're discovering about being loved by God.

I'm loved, yet I'm tempted and broken.
I'm loved, so I'm learning to love others more than I love my addictions.
(Tasha)

I'm loved, yet I've been so anxious about everything.
I'm loved, so I have nothing to fear.
(Liz)

I'm loved, yet I'm afraid.
I'm loved, so I'm discovering courageousness.
(Rachael)

I'm loved, yet I don't know how to love.
I'm loved, so I believe that anything is possible.
(Lizzie)

I'm loved, yet I forget it so quickly.
I'm loved, so I don't have to run any more.
(Susie)

I'm loved, yet sometimes I don't reflect the cost of that love.
I'm loved, so I need not live in the shame of my past.
(Micah)

How will *you* finish both these sentences?

I'm loved, yet . . .
I'm loved, so . . .

I love these words written by David over 3,000 years ago. Use them to focus your heart on Father God. He is your strength and shield. You can be brave because you can be sure that Almighty God fights for you and shelters you. We can be like this for others because we have experienced it for ourselves.

Your mighty God is here with you now. Being in his presence is like finding a pool of sunlight streaming through a window. You can sit in the warmth of his presence. You can soak up the strength that comes from knowing you are loved by him. So why not find a bit of light and soak up the warm rays as you soak up God's love?

The Lord always keeps his promises;
he is gracious in all he does.
The Lord helps the fallen
and lifts those bent beneath their loads.
The eyes of all look to you in hope;
you give them their food as they need it.
When you open your hand,
you satisfy the hunger and thirst of every living thing.
The Lord is righteous in everything he does;
he is filled with kindness.
The Lord is close to all who call on him,
yes, to all who call on him in truth.
He grants the desires of those who fear him;
he hears their cries for help and rescues them.
(Psalm 145:13–19 NLT)

4: BE BEQUTIFUL

It's the pits

Right now I have hairy legs.

And armpits.

I'm not wearing any make-up, and my eyebrows are threatening to take over my face. My nails are chipped, my roots are epic, and if someone came to the door right now, I would seriously consider shouting 'not at home!' instead of facing them in this state.

OK, so I'm not naked (you'll be pleased to hear), so said visitor would be unaware of the hairy legs and pits situation. But *I* would know, and on some deeper level, that knowledge makes me feel a little bit unfeminine.

Why?

Even as I'm writing this, I'm feeling guilty for being so shallow. Now I know that I'm more than the number of likes I get on a profile picture. I know that I'm loveable whether I'm toned, bloated, shaved, plucked, waxed or hairy. But I still inhabit a society that screams at me from every magazine cover, billboard poster and advert that female beauty equals young, slim and hair-free. I know it's a beauty ideal that's unrealistic and unkind, but I also know that unless my beauty is rooted in something deeper than how I'm looking on any given day, I will compare myself with poster-girl and find myself lacking.

'Being beautiful takes a lot of hard work,' Zara told me after I once commented on how gorgeous she always looked. 'I have to go through all these rituals and things I do to make sure I look exactly right. I can't just leave the house moments after getting up. Urgh. I'd look horrible. You wouldn't recognize me.'

Of course, I'd recognize her – I know that's not what she meant. But there's something really sad about a beautiful young woman not wanting to be seen by people (including those who love her), unless she meets an ideal she's adopted from an industry that neither knows nor cares about her.

It seems that being beautiful is a project that, whether we like it or not, every woman is signed up for from the moment we're born. Living in a culture that places such a huge amount of importance on beauty increases our risk not only of not really liking ourselves, but also of envying and even disliking other women whose faces and bodies seem to fit. Social media provides countless ways to compare and judge others on their appearance alone. Anonymous, fast and image-driven, it's the perfect vehicle for encouraging us to participate in cruelty towards ourselves and others. Somehow, if someone's image is online, they're fair game.

The beauty project

Women at war over their image is nothing new. Although the range of beauty products was pretty limited, the women of the past were nonetheless highly creative. Queen Cleopatra of Egypt (69 – 30BC) is recorded as having worn red lipstick made from finely crushed carmine beetles mixed with ants' eggs. Women in Ancient Greece kept the bloom in their cheeks by painting on herbal pastes made from crushed berries and seeds.

By the Middle Ages, wearing make-up was seen as a bit promiscuous, but Queen Elizabeth reclaimed the practice by popularizing the 'natural' look. This involved women at court plastering white lead paste called ceruse all over their faces (which made their hair fall out), and painting their cheeks and lips with red concoctions that permanently stained their skin.

Nice.

Although our understanding of the chemicals involved in cosmetics is superior today, we are possibly just as easily led by society's ideas of beauty as were our ancient sisters. A recent study of English women revealed that when it came to emotional stability, social confidence, self-esteem and physical attractiveness, the women who wore make-up regularly scored lower in these four categories than those who never wore it at all. Wearing make-up seems to make us need to wear make-up.

Making women look 'beautiful' has always been on the cards, but today it's big business. From the cradle to the grave, we have to deal with the ugly truth that being who we are isn't enough. In a world that is hugely critical about how women look, can we really blame the celebrities for giving in to a little nip and tuck to keep themselves in the public eye? Well, in a word, yes. Because the impossible standard of ascetic beauty that these women set soon becomes the benchmark that we are all expected to live up to.

Fashion magazines regularly name and shame the latest celebrity to go under the knife, but who knows whether this is actually true? And that's the other problem, isn't it? Not only are we suspicious of our own bodies for doing what comes 'naturally' (like sprouting hair, sagging and wrinkling), but we are increasingly suspicious that other women are getting a little help to keep up the illusion of perfection. It seems today that if you can get some help to be the most perfect possible version of yourself, you do so, and you're expected to do so too.

It's little wonder if you and I judge ourselves so harshly on what we see in the mirror.

Raw

It's amazing just how many of us feel we fall short of the beauty ideal we have in our minds. Have you ever struggled to leave the house make-up free, or felt that a new outfit would not only boost your self-confidence but also your worth in other people's eyes? You might even be someone who others look at and think, 'She looks so confident; she wouldn't ever be unhappy with how she looks.'

But you are.

And you're not alone.

I haven't always had an easy relationship with my looks. In my late teens I felt uncomfortable with my body, and I spent a lot of my teenage years feeling inferior to other girls, often feeling like a stranger in my own body. If only I had the time, skill and money to 'work on it', things would be better; I would be happier and more confident. The older I got, the more I viewed my body as my project that I had to improve. Sometimes my triggers were being with those people who I thought were far more gorgeous than me. Other times, my triggers were being with people who thought I was beautiful!

I had a lovely relative who would always comment on how nice I looked. I was flattered, and it was really kindly meant. But after a while I began to feel an incredible pressure to make sure that when I saw this relative, I looked the best I could. I was afraid that anything less would be letting her down!

In her disarmingly honest blog, Lisa Hickey paints a painful picture of her self-confessed beauty addiction that is getting in the way of her really living.

> Here we go again, *I think, as I impatiently wait for the hair straightener to warm up. I've washed my hair, deep conditioned it, shaved my legs, tweezed my eyebrows. I've blown dry my hair, but it's still a wreck. It's always a wreck. It's thin, so thin that when I put it into a ponytail, a pencil is thicker. I plaster down the worst of the fly-aways with a hair product that promises something it can't deliver.*
> *What I really want to be doing – instead of going through that same-same ritual – is learning to write code. Studying analytics. Talking with someone halfway round the world about real oppression. Not the kind of oppression that I feel because of my addiction to beauty.*[7]

Relentlessly pursuing a beauty ideal increases our vulnerability to inhabiting a heightened state of self-consciousness, self-doubt and self-criticism. When we worship the idol of beauty, we quickly embrace a very distorted and dissatisfied self-image. Even if many of us know that we will never achieve the beauty ideal for very long, we still seem to be prepared to pay the price financially and emotionally.

Is this really God's best for us – that our value is only derived from this small area of our lives?

Is there a way out?

If you find yourself caught in a cycle of trying to live up to a physical perfection you can never hope to achieve or sustain (because you're a person, not a poster), then it's time to break free and discover how to love the beauty you already are.

But don't panic! The answer isn't throwing out your make-up bag or wearing clothes made out of felt! It lies in working out what beauty is, and what it isn't. If the most beautiful you will ever be is the 'you' that God is moulding and shaping into the likeness of his Son, then chasing anything other than this will always disappoint. God created beauty. It's his gift to his world.

In fact, you don't actually have to 'do' anything to be beautiful to God. He sees his Son Jesus in you if you believe in him. Nothing tops that!

But maybe at the times when we think we're chasing a beauty ideal, we're

actually pursuing something altogether different? Something that's the very opposite of real beauty?

Glamour gullible

You and I operate in a society that has reduced beauty to glamour – and glamour is all about what happens on the surface of our skin. 'This world of glamour caters for the surface and external reality. Once you've got the upfront hit from glamour, you usually find little or nothing behind it.'[8]

If glamour is the blusher painted onto your face, beauty is the inner radiance that lights you up from the inside.

If glamour is the outfit that helps you make an entrance, beauty is your generous heart that means your presence changes the atmosphere.

If glamour is the perfume clinging to your clothes, beauty is the fragrance of your life that lingers long after you've left the room.

God will always be more impressed with your desire for beauty than with your pursuit of glamour. His creativity pulsating through us inspires us to have fun with the glamour, but he calls us into the deeper, richer place of moulding an inner life of hidden beauty that will radiate through our whole being.

In the Old Testament, the prophet Samuel knows that he needs to anoint the next king of Israel. His choices have been narrowed down to the sons from one particular family. God knows that although Samuel is a godly guy, he's still a human being, and will probably be swayed by the 'glamour' he sees, not by the beauty he senses. So he focuses Samuel's attention on the heart with these words: 'God judges persons differently than humans do. Men and women look at the face; God looks into the heart' (1 Samuel 16:7 MSG).

Face lift

This understanding of beauty doesn't negate our need to accept and love our faces and bodies. It doesn't prevent us from exploring different ways to express ourselves through fashion, or undermine our interest in having beauty products and regimes. But what it does do is continually remind us that faces lifted to Jesus will always radiate our true beauty beneath the glamour.

So the right question for us as Christian women to ask ourselves isn't: 'Is it OK to love fashion and wear make-up?', but 'How can we be women who allow our beauty to change the world?'

Wow!

Of course your beauty can change things!

Brave beauty

Invariably, if you hear a talk at a Christian event about beauty and femininity, someone will mention Esther. And why not? She was beautiful and brave. A winning combination. But her story, although deeply powerful, can feel so far away from our daily experience as to make her seem like a fantasy.

The reality is that in her society, she was considered as nothing. Being a woman, a foreigner and an orphan was not a winning combination. But her beauty made her stand out. And it propelled her into the bed and courts of a violent and powerful king who thought nothing of discarding his wife and queen (Vashti) who dared to speak up against the injustice of being paraded in front of a room full of noblemen.

Esther's beauty may have secured her the prize, but being chosen for your body, married to a cruel man and kept for sex is hardly a fairy-tale ending. But incredibly, just as the story darkens with the announcement of the plan to massacre the Jews, Esther steps into the limelight, bold and beautiful. She was beautiful in a brutal place. Hers isn't a story of a cute girl winning a king's heart at a pageant. Hers is a story of courage under fire in saving an ethnic group from annihilation. Although put on a pedestal for her beauty, she sought to be beautiful when it mattered most. And she could have been killed for it.

Mordecai sent this reply to Esther: 'Don't think for a moment that because you're in the palace you will escape when all other Jews are killed. If you keep quiet at a time like this, deliverance and relief for the Jews will arise from some other place, but you and your relatives will die. Who knows if perhaps you were made queen for just such a time as this?'

Then Esther sent this reply to Mordecai: 'Go and gather together all the Jews of Susa and fast for me. Do not eat or drink for three days, night or day. My maids and I will do the same. And then, though it is against the law, I will go in to see the king. If I must die, I must die.' So Mordecai went away and did everything as Esther had ordered him.
(Esther 4:13–17 NLT)

What might Esther say to us today? I think she'd encourage us not to seek the beauty that puts us in the limelight, but to seek situations where we can act boldly and beautifully for the sake of others. She'd love this quote by Lupita Nyong'o: 'What is fundamentally beautiful is compassion for yourself and those around you. That kind of beauty enflames the heart and enchants the soul.'[9]

Over the years, realizing that I am God's beloved daughter and heir has brought about a slow but significant shift in how I see and express myself. My ideas about what is beautiful in another person, even in myself, have changed. For so long I tried not to be vain and insecure about my appearance. What helped was putting down in writing my own personal rally cry to chase the beauty of a Jesus-shaped life rather than the glamour of a magazine-shaped self-image.

My beauty manifesto

I have come up with a list of eight things that I will believe or do, with the help of God, to live a beautiful life.

1. **I am human-being shaped, not magazine-shaped.** So I will start with accepting the body I have, not the body I think I should have.

   Reflection:

   > *Oh yes, you shaped me first inside, then out;*
   >   *you formed me in my mother's womb.*
   > *I thank you, High God – you're breathtaking!*
   >   *Body and soul, I am marvelously made!*
   >   *I worship in adoration – what a creation!*
   > (Psalm 139:13–14 MSG)

2. **I am perfectly imperfect.** So I won't despair when I get spots, wrinkles, or bloated around my period. The people who truly love me, love the whole lot. Genuinely! Instead of obsessing with the things I'd like to tweak or do over, I'll focus on my inner life and how beautiful that is becoming.

Reflection:

> *You should clothe yourselves instead with the beauty that comes from within, the unfading beauty of a gentle and quiet spirit, which is so precious to God.*
> (1 Peter 3:4 NLT)

3. **I'll dress to express, not to impress.** So what I wear has to fit my shape, not just my body shape, but the person God is helping me to become.

Reflection:

> *So we have stopped evaluating others from a human point of view. At one time we thought of Christ merely from a human point of view. How differently we know him now! This means that anyone who belongs to Christ has become a new person. The old life is gone; a new life has begun!*
> (2 Corinthians 5:16–17 NLT)

4. **My body is my companion, not my project.** So keeping my body reasonably healthy and clean is being a good steward of God's gift.

Reflection:

> *So here's what I want you to do, God helping you: Take your everyday, ordinary life – your sleeping, eating, going-to-work, and walking-around life – and place it before God as an offering.*
> (Romans 12:1 MSG)

5. **I will appreciate my body for what it does, not just for what it looks like.** I am called to serve the will of God. This involves my body: comforting people, going places, sitting with someone trapped in hopelessness. It's not the size of my boobs or the whiteness of my smile that has the greatest impact on hurting lives.

Reflection:

> *Charm can mislead and beauty soon fades.*
>   *The woman to be admired and praised*
>   *is the woman who lives in the Fear-of-GOD.*
> (Proverbs 31:30 MSG)

6. **I will chase beauty, not glamour.** So I'll limit the amount of air-time I give fashion magazines and shopping trips, because I know that, unchecked, these can rob me of valuing a beautiful heart over a perfect face. I want

Jesus to open my eyes to the true beauty that comes from surrendering myself to him.

Reflection:

> *Your eyes are windows into your body. If you open your eyes wide in wonder and belief, your body fills up with light. If you live squinty-eyed in greed and distrust, your body is a dank cellar. If you pull the blinds on your windows, what a dark life you will have!*
> (Matthew 6:22–23 MSG)

> *Cultivate inner beauty, the gentle, gracious kind that God delights in. The holy women of old were beautiful before God that way . . .*
> (1 Peter 3:4–5 MSG)

7. **I will live from the inside out, focusing on God first.** So I'm signed up for God's plan for my life and won't opt out of doing what he asks because I am self-absorbed about how I look, or held back by my fears and insecurities.

Reflection:

> *Focusing on the self is the opposite of focusing on God. Anyone completely absorbed in self ignores God, ends up thinking more*

about self than God. That person ignores who God is and what he is doing. And God isn't pleased at being ignored.
(Romans 8:7–8 MSG)

8. **I will be realistic and positive about myself.** So I'll allow people I trust to help me embrace the real me and challenge the times when I act or dress in ways that don't fit with who I am.

Reflection:

God brings [grace] to you. The only accurate way to understand ourselves is by what God is and by what he does for us, not by what we are and what we do for him.
(Romans 12:3 MSG)

Be beautiful

There's something liberating about revolting against the mainstream! This is what Esther did. It's what makes her story ageless. There have been other beautiful women whose names have gone down in history: Cleopatra, Helen of Troy, Marie Antoinette, Marilyn Monroe; the list goes on. But none of these women demonstrated the great truth that the most beautiful you will ever be is when you dare to lose everything for the sake of others.

Above everything you choose to wear, or do to your face or body, remember this: I passionately believe the most beautiful you will ever be is when you love others. When you lay down your rights, status and dreams for the sake of the lost, the last and the least.

Desire to be the real you. Even if there are parts of your body that don't work well or look as you think they should. The truth is that you are fantastically you: incomparable and mysterious. Don't compare your flesh-and-blood loveliness with the perfection of the static paper girls you see online or in a magazine. Seek the opportunities to 'do' beautiful, not the platforms to be beautiful. If you're inhaling the smoke of glamour and wondering why you're choking, get outside and breathe in the truth that you are beautifully and wonderfully made. When you do that, you'll be arrested by the sheer beauty you see in and around you.

And you'll want more of it.

When you look in the mirror, look *for* yourself, not simply *at* yourself. Look for love; look for compassion; look for openness, trustworthiness, hope. Look for courage in the face of trouble. Look for peace. Then let others see this beauty too.

The goal of glamour is to make everyone feel envious. The goal of beauty is to make everyone feel loved.

As you paint your nails (or not!), love the hands God gave you to reach out to others and shape this world. As you get your slap on (or not!), love the endless ways your face expresses the joys and sorrows in your heart. As you get your trainers or heels on, love the body that takes you on endless adventures in God's world.

Chase Beauty, and change the world!

Wonderland

1. Has your freedom as a Western woman to control your looks ever controlled you?
2. When you look at your body in the mirror, what do you think or feel?
3. How much do you think about, worry about, obsess about your appearance?
4. How can you be loyal to the face God has given you? What can you do to make sure that your use of make-up and fashion complements, rather than hides, who you are?
5. What are some of your beauty triggers? It might help to chat with someone about them to see if there are any practical steps you can take to make a difference, for example, limiting the number of fashion magazines you read, asking yourself questions about the beauty ideal you feel compared to: 'Has this image been airbrushed?'; 'Who says this is what I need to look like?'

6. Who, or what, are some of the 'anchors' in your life who help you appreciate yourself?
7. What 'roots' your beauty? If you see your beauty as coming from the shape of your figure and face, how can you begin to see it coming from your loving heart and generous attitude?

My sanctuary

We often compare ourselves to others and, more often than not, find ourselves wanting. Comparison kills confidence because it stops us from seeing that we are our own standard of beauty. It also makes us deny the inevitable, that over time our bodies will change. If you think this will make you unlovable, it's inevitable that you might one day end up hating yourself and pushing people who love you away.

Find a photo of yourself and think about the critical things you think about your face/body/image. Imagine that person in the photo was your best friend, or daughter. What would change about how you look at the picture?

Read these beautiful words, and ask God to show you what else you have about you that he considers as your beauty that will only increase with time:

Get off the scales! I have yet to see a scale that can tell you how enchanting your eyes are. I have yet to see a scale that can show you how wonderful your hair looks when the sun shines its glorious rays on it. I have yet to see a scale that can thank you for your compassion, sense of humour, and contagious smile. Get off the scale because I have yet to see one that can admire you for your perseverance when challenged in life. It's true, the scale can only give you a numerical reflection of your relationship with gravity. That's it. It cannot measure beauty, talent, purpose, life force, possibility, strength or love. Don't give the scale more power than it has earned. Take note of the number, then get off the scale and live your life. You are beautiful![10]

5: BE REAL

The sexiest thing in the entire world is being really smart. And being thoughtful. And being generous. Everything else is [rubbish]! I promise you! It's just [rubbish] that people try to sell to you to make you feel like less. So don't buy it. Be smart, be thoughtful, and be generous.
Ashton Kutcher

Have you ever seen a naked nun?

Years ago I went on holiday to France with a rag-tag bunch of mates. Without wanting to sound like a *Friends* episode, we were an atheist, a businessman, a busker, an art student, a youth worker (me) and an ex-nun (Mel).

We'd known Mel for a few years. She'd only just left the convent (in her mid-twenties), so this holiday was a way to ease her into life 'on the outside'. It was April: cold, dreary and wet. On the first day we all headed off to a beach to chuck some stones in the sea. Suddenly, out from behind a rock, Mel appeared, completely naked! Arms flailing in the air, and whooping her head off, she ran into the sea.

We stood there, totally transfixed, staring as she threw herself into the waves, and then came up spluttering and laughing.

My friend, Tom, the atheist, turned to me. 'She's not a nun any more?'

'No,' I laughed.

'But she's still religious, right? But she doesn't look very religious.'

'She looks very real though,' I murmured, deeply moved at my friend's joy. It was one of the most sexual things I have ever witnessed in my life.

Talking about anything to do with sex requires a few definitions. Being sexual and having sex are very different things. Having sex is what you do. Being sexual is who you are. On that beach in France, I didn't see Mel having sex or being sexually flirtatious. What I saw was my friend celebrating herself as

a physical and sexual being. Splashing around naked in the freezing cold sea made her feel alive, free and glad to be a woman!

Sex-y-you

God made you a sexual being. You have a God-created sexuality.

It's not to do with whether or not you've had or ever will have sex. It's not even primarily about who you feel sexually attracted to (sexual orientation), or the decisions you make about if or when you will have sex (sexual morality). Here are some of the things that are included when we talk about sexuality:

1. **Female sex** – how we feel about, and treat, our sexual body parts
2. **Gender identity** – how we handle and express being female
3. **Gender role** – the ideas we embrace or reject about how we should behave because we are female
4. **Sexual orientation** – who we're sexually attracted to (heterosexual, homosexual or bisexual)
5. **Body image** – how we physically express ourselves or allow others to treat our bodies in a relationship, online or in public
6. **Sexual experiences** – how we act in response to our sexual thoughts, ideas and fantasies
7. **Relationship experiences** – how we demonstrate intimacy, love, compassion, joy and sadness to others.

It's no wonder then that sexuality can be such a complicated subject. It covers so many things! From now on, when I talk about 'female sexuality', it's this complete list that I'm referring to. You won't be surprised by the number of young Christian women I talk to who feel conflicted about how they should handle their female sexuality.

'I want to explore my body to know myself better, but isn't masturbation a sin?' (Chloe)

'I have sexual thoughts, but can't work out which ones could be OK in God's eyes and which ones are too shameful to share.' (Hollie)

'Last year my boyfriend dumped me because he felt I was too big a sexual temptation for him. He couldn't cope with the lustful thoughts he had about me. On bad days I'm still convinced that being me is such a sin that I'm not good enough to marry a godly guy.' (Alice)

'I honestly don't know what I feel. These aches come over me for someone or something. I'm worried that I might just one day give in and do something I know I shouldn't.' (Tia)

'I desperately want sex. I'm not sure why or even with whom! Ideally, I'd like to wait for marriage, but that seems ludicrous in this day and age.' (Emily)

You may have read a book or heard a talk about what God thinks about sexual penetration. But did you realize that he has so much wisdom, grace and strength to offer you for all the rest too? He's the Maker with the manual.

I am woman

The first and most important thing you need to know is that your female sexuality is a good gift from God. He loves the fact that you're a woman.

Your femaleness matters:

Your body made of skin, bone, blood and sinew; your lungs filled with God-breath so that you can build, create and connect; your nervous system, hormones, emotions and thought patterns; your sexual organs and erogenous zones with their capacity for profound and intense sexual pleasure; your ability to experience intimacy, desire, love, compassion, joy and sorrow – all of this matters to God.

He sculpted you from nothingness into womanliness, and the psalmist reckons that your existence is an utter miracle.

> *I thank you, High God – you're breathtaking!*
> *Body and soul, I am marvelously made!*
> (Psalm 139:14 MSG)

So you need to discover the woman God made you to be, because God put so much into creating all of you.

Just like Eve.

Genesis tells the story of earth's first-ever human female. She bursts onto the scene naked, strong and pulsing with the promise of new life. She has a vagina where Adam has a penis. Breasts where Adam has a chest. Womb, fallopian tubes, curves, dimples, hopes, passion, energy, desire: she's the same as Adam, but vastly different. She fits with him, and he with her. But she also stands before God, alone.

The man said,

'This is now bone of my bones
*   and flesh of my flesh;*
she shall be called "woman",
*   for she was taken out of man.'*

That is why a man leaves his father and mother and is united to his wife, and they become one flesh.
*   Adam and his wife were both naked, and they felt no shame.*
(Genesis 2:23–25 NIV)

I am responsible

As well as your female sexuality being a good gift, it's also a real responsibility.

Just like guys can find their male sexuality hard to handle sometimes, being female can also be challenging and complicated. Before we think about the struggles we face, let's have a moment to consider the lads. In my book *The Dating Dilemma*, a great friend called Andy opened up about the fragility of the male ego.

> *The male ego is very vulnerable; it's just that we don't show it or we protect it in confrontational ways. We need girls to bring us out of ourselves, not to be constantly putting us down. We're looking for a girlfriend who is a friend that we can open up to more than we can to our mates. That's the amazing gift that girls give to us guys ... I believe that this is what we're really searching for when we ask you out – a place of intimacy. Unfortunately, sex is the only place of intimacy we see in lad culture, and mostly it's not about intimacy but performance. Without sounding soppy, I think the connection we find with the girl we date and fall in love with is like finding home.*
> (Andy)[11]

Our God-given desire for connection with others means that we are capable of experiencing deep empathy, compassion, passion and intimacy. These things are crucial not just for romantic relationships, but for living a meaningful life. But these same tools can be misused and manipulated by us and others. I remember going clubbing with a friend who had just experienced a horrible break-up. I was shocked at the way some men seemed to make a beeline for her, sensing her fragility and hunger to feel better about herself.

It also doesn't help that we receive conflicting messages about how we should handle our female sexuality. On the one hand, we're sometimes made to feel ashamed of having female bodies or sexual desires. While at Bible college, an older, popular male student announced that 'men might be on a diet, but they still look at the menu, so could the female students stop wearing skinny jeans?' Although the student in question probably had good and honourable motives in making his comment, and we thought it rather funny, our little group of younger girls, all struggling with low self-esteem, felt that everyone just saw us as sex objects. Sexualized comments, or churches and families who remain silent about sex, tend to create cultures of shame and secrecy around the whole area of sexuality.

Then, on the other hand, we're bombarded by the pornified, super-enhanced female bodies with big breasts, hair-free vaginas, long legs and firm stomachs that we're supposed to emulate. When a culture is saturated with these images, people tend to believe that they must be the real thing. We may regularly see a celebrity's near-naked body on Twitter, but we'll never get to see the real woman without the masks of her heavily orchestrated sex appeal. We're meant to desire her or envy her, not know her.

Both the sex-silent church and the sex-saturated culture contribute to a distorted view of what it means to be a real woman. For those of us who want to embrace and express our female sexuality in God-honouring ways, it can feel bewildering, to say the least.

I am real

Time for a bit of honesty.

Throughout my teens and twenties I was determined to submit my female sexuality to God. I wanted to be available to him, whether that meant getting married or being single all my life. If I dated a guy, I would become crippled with guilt and shame if our kissing led us anywhere further than a platonic peck on the cheek! I felt that God was testing me at every turn – and it was a test that I was failing. After one particularly physical relationship, I developed a masturbation habit as a way to feel better about myself. I felt miserable, but unable to stop. Convinced that God was mad at me, I stopped asking him to help me have a healthy view of my sexual awakening. I began to hate my body, and either flaunted it to get the attention I craved, or punished it by overeating or starving myself.

I was desperate to find a Christian woman who seemed to have this nailed. But no-one seemed up for being real with me. This forced me into thinking I needed to look more than sorted, to hide what was really happening. It took me years to realize that the solution wasn't stopping masturbating. The freedom came when I asked God to show me the unmet needs and desires I was trying to meet by masturbating.

Jess wanted to be the leader and preacher God was raising her up to be. But she was addicted to watching porn. It was a dark secret that plagued her life, and she hated it and hated herself for being so 'weak'. Any time she was in a discussion about sex, she made her views on not dating, kissing or even praying together before marriage very clear: 'All forms of intimacy before marriage are just too dangerous. I just don't even think about these things any more; they're beneath me.' Friends admired her purity; Jess hated her hypocrisy.

One of the problems with having thoughts and feelings that make us feel dirty, ashamed or unable to break out of damaging habits is that we may end up fixating on the sexual sin instead of the God who can free us. As long as your sin and not God is at the centre of your thinking, you'll find ways to punish yourself, convinced that you're bad, and God can't love you. A young woman I prayed with about her addiction to masturbation wrote to me later,

I ended up in a mess, convinced that I was dirty, convinced that God couldn't love me. And the very thing I hated myself for doing became the very thing I turned to as a way to medicate my pain. I had to masturbate to comfort myself, then loathed myself for being so obsessed with when I could next be on my own to do it. In the process, I began to harbour the belief that not only was sex bad, but being sexual tainted me too.

What released her from this damaging cycle was the direct work of the Holy Spirit in helping her to be real with herself about the deeper needs she was seeking to meet through sex. Only then could she bring masturbation to God and a trusted friend. She is beginning to experience the difference between feeding a damaging obsession and finding ways to appreciate her own body.

Real, godly sexuality

Often we act out of what we believe.

If we believe that our female sexuality is an embarrassing, or bad, part of us, then we'll try to ignore or deny it. If we believe that our female sexuality is God-given and core to who we are, then we'll be more likely to ask God to help us. A sign of having an authentic female sexuality is being able to be thankful and accountable to God for and in it.

The apostle Paul longed for the new Christians in the city of Corinth to grasp this. Corinth had a reputation in the ancient world as being a bit of a sexual playground. The religion of the day was worship to the goddess Diana. Worship at her temple involved sex with temple prostitutes. It also championed a Greek philosophical dualism which taught that as the spiritual life is more important than the physical life, you can do whatever you want with your body or other people's bodies. After all, sex is just sex – if you want it, have it. Right? 'No!' says Paul. In his letter to the Corinthian church, he knocks this thinking out of the park. But instead of starting with what they can or can't do now they are Christians (sexual morality), Paul reminds them of who they are (sexual identity), before challenging them to live radically (sexual potential). Read what he says:

In the past, some of you were like that, but you were washed clean. You were made holy, and you were made right with God in the name of the Lord Jesus Christ and in the Spirit of our God.

'I am allowed to do all things,' but not all things are good for me to do. 'I am allowed to do all things,' but I will not let anything make me its slave . . . Surely you know that your bodies are parts of Christ himself. So I must never take the parts of Christ and join them to a prostitute! It is written in the Scriptures, 'The two will become one body.' . . . You should know that your body is a temple for the Holy Spirit who is in you. You have received the Holy Spirit from God. So you do not belong to

yourselves, because you were bought by God for a price. So honor God with your bodies.
(1 Corinthians 6:11–20 NCV)

Remember

1. We are free (verse 11)

You don't get yourself sorted out sexually so that you can be free. You have already been set free by Jesus, so you don't need to be afraid that your sexual experiences, thoughts and feelings will make you unacceptable to God. Paul says that when you receive Jesus as Lord, you are 'washed clean'. You are a beautiful new creation, not a patched-up old one. This means that you are free to be brutally real with yourself and God about where your sexuality struggles are enslaving you. Ask yourself:

- Do I ever feel inadequate as a woman? If so, how do I compensate?
- Do I ever have sexual experiences that leave me ashamed or unable to seek support or help?
- Am I restricted by other people's expectations of what I can do, or achieve, as a young woman? How do I respond?
- If I'm struggling to be free from habitual masturbation, watching porn, premarital sex and so on, what one thing can I do to demonstrate that I desire to be free more than I desire to meet my sexual urge?

- Who can I share my desire for sexual freedom with? How might they be able to support me to step into freedom rather than remain trapped by sin?

2. *We are vulnerable (verse 12)*

You are free, but this doesn't mean that you're not vulnerable to being enslaved again. Paul reminds the Corinthians that although they are free, they are to be responsible for staying free. This means recognizing those times when you're more likely to give in to temptation or believe lies that hold you back. Ask yourself:

- What temptations do I struggle most to resist?
- When do I sense I'm misusing my own or someone else's sexuality (e.g. being emotionally manipulative to get my own way, or being deliberately sexually flirtatious to make myself feel good)?
- What, and who, are the triggers for this kind of behaviour?
- Does anyone have undue and negative influence over how I see myself and my calling as a woman?
- Am I prone to thinking that sex is bad? Who could I talk to about this in order to help me have a healthy view of sex and my female sexuality?
- Is there a woman to whom I can open up about my vulnerabilities?

3. We are God's (verses 15, 19-20)

The whole of you belongs to God, including your sexual desires, orientation and hopes. God doesn't own you like a possession for him to use and discard. His sense of ownership of you is about him wanting the very best for you. He knows what's good and right for you, and what will hurt and damage you. He knows that you can honour him in how you express your female sexuality – and he wants to teach you how!

Ask yourself:

- When did I last thank God for my female sexuality?
- Am I open to healthy compliments? Can I tell the difference between these and people trying to flatter me to get what they want?
- Do I know how to protect myself when people want to treat me in a sexualized way? (For example, if a man keeps drawing unwanted attention to what I'm wearing or my looks, do I just laugh or do I hold my ground?)
- Am I open to being challenged about how I express myself through fashion and body language?
- If I feel that God is calling me to a certain career/situation/position, what's stopping me from pursuing that?
- Am I able to imagine having a sexual relationship in marriage that's full of faithful, exciting, adventurous sex?

4. *We have great sexual potential (verse 16)*

Paul knows that God only gives good gifts, and sexuality is a very good gift with inbuilt blessings. Vaginal penetration (what we often refer to as 'sex') can lead to having babies. But the blessings of being sexual aren't limited to reproduction. You could remain sexually celibate all your life and still reach your sexual potential – because it's got nothing to do with your relationship status. When we're single, we can often feel excluded from sex talks in church or relationship chats with peers, which all tend to be about the difficulties of dating someone and saving sex until marriage. It's true that the 'one flesh' Paul talks about is a man and a woman being united in sexual intimacy. But this is meant to be a reflection of the intimate love God has for us. You are experiencing your sexual potential when you give yourself fully to Jesus. Being single gives you a unique opportunity to explore this. Ask yourself:

- Am I allowing my relationship status to dictate whether or not I'm living a full life?
- What blessings am I already experiencing (intimate times with a good friend or being able to empathize with a stranger)?
- How am I investing in my key friendships?

5. *We always have a choice (verse 18)*

Paul doesn't present his case for God-honouring sexuality and then leave the Corinthians clueless as to what to do next. He gives them a compelling vision of living free from sexual sin, and a very effective exit strategy for situations that would jeopardize that: 'RUN!'

You can always make a choice as to whether to continue doing what you're doing or get out of there. Sometimes we overcome sin by standing our ground and facing the cold hard truth of why we always end up in sexual situations that we know aren't right for us. But sometimes we overcome sin by knowing when we need the power of flight: we just know that to protect ourselves and others, we need to get out of there, and fast. Ask yourself:

- Is there anything that I need to run from?
- What am I filling my heart and mind with? How do I 'run away' from images of unhealthy sexuality?
- What exit strategies could I establish to help me in situations where I might become enslaved again?

Really loved

So far in this chapter, our conversation around sexuality has focused on being female. But often when people use the term 'sexuality', they're referring to

sexual orientation. The four types of sexual orientation are: heterosexual (erotically attracted to the opposite sex), homosexual (erotically attracted to the same sex), bisexual (erotically attracted to both sexes) and transgender (someone who crosses culturally defined categories for sex and gender).[12]

Questioning how to reconcile a same-sex orientation with a love of Jesus can make a person feel immensely vulnerable to being rejected by their family, church and God. Tragically, some Christians have experienced rejection when they 'came out' as gay, or expressed their struggles with same-sex attraction. This is appalling and deeply sad. No-one should ever face rejection or discrimination from God's people. When Bethany 'came out' to me, I could hardly hear what she was saying because her fear that she might be rejected by God and the church she loved with all her heart was making her throw up. I was crying too as I held back her hair from her face, and listened to the years of fear and isolation pouring out of her.

The truth is that God's unfathomable love for us is unchanging, regardless of our sexual orientation or sexual experiences. If you're struggling with questions surrounding your own sexual orientation, remember that you are standing before a loving Father who calls you his beloved – your sexual orientation doesn't change that.

But maybe, like Bethany, you're discovering that there are no easy answers. It can be confusing that Christians hold different views about whether the

Bible supports gay relationships or not. Some Christians are convinced that faithful, monogamous gay relationships are blessed by God. Others are convinced that while everyone is accepted by God, there is a clear pattern for sexual relationships in the Bible between one man and one woman, so anything else is not part of God's original design for human sexual relationships.

Jesus never talked explicitly about sexual orientation. In fact, there are a number of sex-related things that he didn't mention at all: abortion, same-sex marriage, masturbation and premarital sex, for example. He addressed things like injustice, greed and pride more than sex. So when he did talk about sex, it really matters what he said. What we see is that he points to God's design for sexual intimacy as being between a man and a woman (Matthew 19:4–5).

Whenever I chat with Bethany about what Jesus says about sex, she astounds me with her honesty and trust: 'I want to be single for a while and work out what God's plan for my life is. I think it will be hard not ever to be with someone, but I want to honour God.'

Whether or not you agree with Bethany's choice to come out as gay and choose celibacy, it's important to give yourself time and space to be real with yourself and trusted friends or mentors. Following Jesus isn't about wearing masks to make people think we are who we're not. That's empty religion,

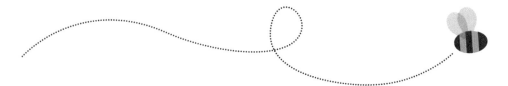

and God wants none of it. He's after a real relationship with you. What he longs for is that you invite him into this area of struggle and pain, trusting that he will lovingly lead you in ways that bring into your life more abundance than you could ever dream of. Writing to the Ephesians, Paul challenges them to raise their vision: 'God can do anything, you know – far more than you could ever imagine or guess or request in your wildest dreams! He does it not by pushing us around but by working within us, his Spirit deeply and gently within us' (Ephesians 3:20 MSG).

I know that when I depend on God and am challenged to go beyond what I think I can do in my own strength, I experience him helping me in the struggles I have with the different aspects of my female sexuality, and this leads me into a deeper relationship with him. This is my hope for you too.

Whatever your journey looks like, whatever your struggles, never lose sight of his goodness and your belovedness. This is the only place to start these big conversations.

God knows

So many of the incredible stories in the Bible are told without commentary. Sometimes we know what God thinks about someone's actions; other times we don't. Bathsheba's story is one of those.

One late afternoon, David got up from taking his nap and was strolling on the roof of the palace. From his vantage point on the roof he saw a woman bathing. The woman was stunningly beautiful. David sent to ask about her, and was told, 'Isn't this Bathsheba, daughter of Eliam and wife of Uriah the Hittite?' David sent his agents to get her. After she arrived, he went to bed with her. (This occurred during the time of 'purification' following her period.) Then she returned home. Before long she realized she was pregnant.
(2 Samuel 11:2–5 MSG)

We know that David gets into trouble for his part in the affair. But what about her part? Rejecting the sexual advances of a king, even though she was married to one of his commanders, may have put her at serious risk. She may have felt she had no choice but to consent. But maybe she planned to be naked in the sight of the palace? Or perhaps she was genuinely bowled over by being the object of desire of a powerful man, and hoped it would lead to love? Who knows?

One thing we do know, though, is that God knew. He knows us: our hearts, our motives, our choices and our struggles. He knows when we're struggling to see our sexuality as a good gift that can honour him, or when we're at risk of hurting ourselves and others. What he's looking for is the willing heart that seeks above all things to honour him.

Sometimes our perception of the women in the Bible can suffer from the layers of cultural and theological cladding that have been set up around them. Famous women are often unkindly categorized as either saint or sinner, nun or slut. The tragedy for us is that we can miss the moments when they chose to be shaped by God, rather than their environment of self-doubt.

I think there's one such moment at the beginning of two of the Gospels. It involves Mary.

Now, I've often overlooked Mary, the mother of Jesus. I've assumed that as she was chosen by God to bear his Son, somehow she was inherently different from me. But although a daughter of her time, she was still a daughter of God, who was chosen, among other things, because she was able simply to accept what God asked of her. She didn't brag or boast; she didn't seek status as a result of her new situation; or even fight for her right to have her name 'cleared'. She saw her femaleness as a gift from God, to be used as he chose. And this was his choice for her:

> *Yes, I see it all now:*
> *I'm the Lord's maid, ready to serve.*
> *Let it be with me*
> *just as you say.*
> (Luke 1:38 MSG)

Be real

Of course, there will never be another mother of God.

But you and I are made of the same stuff as Mary. She was flesh and blood, skin and sinew, with hopes and fears just like ours. Loving our sexuality and offering ourselves fully and freely to God opens us up to the fullness of life that Christ promises. Who knows what God might do in you as you make your very sexuality available to him to guide and use for his glory? Who knows what impact it might have on others who feel so confused or broken by their own, or other people's, misuse of sexuality?

So, any time you feel tempted to hide away your struggles, or take on a sexual self-image that you know isn't real, run!

Your sexuality is a gift to you from a loving God who made you to be real. Your desires for connection and intimacy are a gift that you are responsible for. Once we grab hold of this, we can begin to be realistic about our sexuality, and create boundaries and opportunities that enable us to live out our glorious female sexuality for the glory of his name.

Wonderland

1. How do you feel about your female sexuality?
2. How do you express yourself sexually? Make a list of ways you:
   express yourself creatively
   demonstrate your emotions
   communicate with others
   respond to intimate situations.
3. What aspects of being sexual are you enjoying right now, and what are you struggling with?
4. Sometimes naming our struggles can be our incentive to seek the help we need. What could your next step be in finding your way through these struggles to a deeper love of God and the freedom he gives?
5. Where do you feel you need to be taking more responsibility for your sexuality?
6. Bathsheba and Mary present very different stories about women's sexuality. Who are the women in your life who express to you a God-honouring sexuality that you want to emulate?
7. Could you arrange to spend some time chatting with them about some of the choices, mistakes and blessings they're experiencing as sexual beings?

My sanctuary

Go outside and find a leaf. Choose the first one that appeals to you. Then find a quiet spot and study it. Really look at it. Let your eyes wander over its shape and structure, taking in all the tiny details you don't normally notice.

It's brilliant, isn't it? And it's just a leaf!

Do you ever contemplate your body like this? You might scrutinize yourself fully clothed, checking that your outfit and image are how you want them to be. But how about naked? Do you ever look at yourself and take in the brilliance of your female body? Presenting our bodies as temples of God's Spirit and not lust objects starts with us choosing to see what God sees, and love what God loves. When you feel brave enough, start naming the different parts of your body, and thank God for them.

'This is my . . . created by God. I'm grateful for it and want to love and respect it.'

This is going to feel like an odd thing to do! But if you can, persevere. It will have a positive impact on how you feel about yourself. When we appreciate and value our bodies, especially our private, sexual parts, we are more empowered in valuing and respecting ourselves in our relationships.

Read these ancient verses and circle words that grab you. As you read over the passage a few times, allow the truth of these words to settle within you.

You made all the delicate, inner parts of my body
*   and knit me together in my mother's womb.*
Thank you for making me so wonderfully complex!
*   Your workmanship is marvellous – how well I know it.*
You watched me as I was being formed in utter seclusion,
*   as I was woven together in the dark of the womb.*
You saw me before I was born.
*   Every day of my life was recorded in your book.*
Every moment was laid out
*   before a single day had passed.*
(Psalm 139:13–16 NLT)

6: BE PURE

The other day, I scrolled my way through thousands of online images of cats. There was a very good reason for this, but I haven't got time to go into details now. You'll just have to take my word for it.

Anyway.

To begin with, the photos were quite cute: fluffy kitten sitting in a flowery mug; two fluffy kittens sitting in a flowery mug; three fluffy kittens – you get the idea. But then, as I immersed myself more and more in the world of people who take photos of their cats and post them online, I began to come across mini horrors. Not-so-fluffy kitten with bloodshot eyes eating flowery mug. Even more ugly kitten throttling another kitten in a flowery mug. The more I looked, the less I liked what I saw (and to be honest, the more nervous I felt about cat lovers!).

But cats aside, there's a word in Christian discipleship that can start sounding nice to begin with, and end up taking us to weird places in our heads. And that word is 'purity'.

What comes to mind when you think of purity?

Fluffy kittens in cups?

Someone who doesn't have sex?

Someone who doesn't want to have sex, ever?

Someone who no-one else wants to have sex with?

Isn't it interesting that the moment we hear the word 'purity', we think of sex? A pure life is about more than how we use our bodies sexually, but it's unsurprising that we tend to think about sex first, because we're surrounded by impure messages about sex all the time. Stories of famous men abusing children, sex scandals in churches, more porn sites clogging up the internet, people sold as sex slaves – all evidence that when we misuse sex, we misuse ourselves and others.

Wild

I remember spending a day with a boyfriend, hiking in the mountains. The weather was brutal: wild, wet, windy. Within seconds of leaving our car, we were soaked through. The further we walked, the wetter we got, and the less we cared. We threw our heads back and roared at the elements. We laughed like hyenas, knowing that no-one could hear us, as no-one else was nuts enough to be on the mountain in such bad weather. We felt alone in our universe, wide awake and fearless.

Sometimes sex might offer this kind of intimacy: two people locked together in a love-flood. Secure, ecstatic, fulfilled.

Then we turned a corner, and the wind that was whistling off the mountain took a nasty turn. It caught me up for a brief moment before knocking me back to the ground. It was all so fast that I didn't really know what had happened until I was lying on the shingle, bruised and very cold.

Sometimes sex might offer something painful: hurt from an encounter that knocks people off track and leaves them with a deeper sense of being alone.

That experience round the lake taught me something about hiking and purity! If you don't want to get knocked off your feet, get behind a tree (or get heavier!).

Love purity

Choosing sexual purity is a way of loving God and valuing his gift of sex.

If we could boil down what the Bible says about sex, it would be: when you are sexually intimate, you lose your old self and find your new self as one with someone else. It's an act of creation in and of itself. Sex is about two people becoming one, and forming the strongest bond outside of God's bond with us. It's a sign to a society saturated by stories of sexual disorder of what being one with God is like.

Jesus spoke in no uncertain terms about why sex God's way was the best way.

> *'Haven't you read,' he replied, 'that at the beginning the Creator "made them male and female," and said, "For this reason a man will leave his father and mother and be united to his wife, and the two will become one flesh"? So they are no longer two, but one flesh. Therefore what God has joined together, let no one separate.'*
> (Matthew 19:4–6 NIV)

The sex act is part of the journey of becoming one that a man and a woman embark on when they choose before God to spend the rest of their lives together. There is something profoundly binding about the sex act: the Greek has 'one flesh', which means to be glued or fused into one being.

One being.

But it's not just the act of sex that produces this oneness. It's the blessing of God over a man and a woman who covenant themselves before him, exclusively and for life, that unites. What God joins together, no-one is to separate.

More

Purity is not just about saving sexual intimacy for marriage; it's a way to face your whole life. Purity is a way of travelling, not a destination, and on the journey we face lots of obstacles.

Take Lucy, for example. She's bisexual, and she loves Jesus. From time to time, she watches gay porn. Because she loves Jesus, she wants to get a handle on the sexual temptations and addictions that she struggles with. She wants to be sexually pure: clean, free, not confused or overwhelmed with guilt any more. So she buys a ring and calls it her purity ring. She decides to wear it on her wedding finger until it's replaced by the real deal when the man of her dreams does the swap.

I know Lucy. She doesn't feel that she can sort herself out, but she's not sure if she trusts God to sort things out either. So what's the role of the purity ring in all of this?

Take Vicky. She's dating James, and they both love Jesus. From time to time they struggle to stick to their 'no-sex-before-marriage' choice. It tends to be when they're in an empty house, or it's late, or one of them has shared something personal, or they've been praying together. Their relationship is healthy: they communicate well and care deeply for each other. Even their mums get along! But they feel like their relationship is on a roller coaster of success and failure. Why is the intimacy that feels so good so wrong?

Take Val. She watches porn, and she loves Jesus. She hasn't told anyone because it feels too shameful. Although she vowed to keep her knickers on when fooling around with her first boyfriend, her resolve dissolved more times that she would like to remember. She's never sought God as much as she has these past few months, so why is this happening?

Each one of these women is experiencing a hunger for purity, but each one is convinced that they don't make the grade. They're confusing purity with inexperience. Sexual purity is a positive choice that we make. In fact, the more we face up to our sexual desires, temptations and experiences, the more we realize what a great and much-needed gift the choice of sexual purity is. Instead

of being defined by our experiences, we can allow them to remind us of how much we need God's Spirit to make us sexually strong.

You can choose purity, even if you have already had sexual experiences or are finding your sexuality difficult to understand.

Chase chastity

Another term used to describe a life of sexual purity is 'chastity'. Put simply, it means not being sexually active (if single), and not being unfaithful (if married). But it's so much more than just that. Chastity is about love. It's about loving as many people as deeply as possible. Just without sex.

This might sound a little odd, and even impossible! We live in such a sexually disorientated society that the thought even of loving someone deeply sounds like code for something sexual.

But as a chaste married woman, I can build deep and safe relationships with male and female friends, because I won't be seeking to become sexually intimate with them. I'm still tuned into my weaknesses, and I make sure I'm wise with how much time I spend alone with someone, or how much of my intimate self I share. But choosing chastity has freed me to be me. In the words of theologian Dietrich Bonhoeffer, 'The essence of chastity is not the suppression of lust, but the total orientation of one's life towards a goal.'[13]

That goal is love.

This understanding of sexual purity changes everything. It's the difference between:

'I'm chaste because I don't believe in sex before marriage.'

And . . .

'I'm chaste because my life's goal is to love everyone.'

Share the love

I believe God desires for you to be chaste if you're not married, and faithful in your marriage if you are, because he wants you to be free to love as deeply and as freely as possible.

Darcey sat with her friends at college as, one by one, everybody shared their 'when-I-lost-my-virginity' story. She didn't have one, so she said nothing. Later she told me how weird she found it: 'We've all been friends since we were twelve, and I couldn't help sitting there thinking, "Aww, they're growing up." Then I thought, "Wait a minute. If they're growing up, then I'm missing out!" And I know I'm not, but it feels like my life is beginning to head off in a different direction because of sex, which is weird!'

We began to chat about how Darcey's choice of chastity didn't mean she now had nothing to say or share with her friends. Quite the opposite, in fact. As we chatted more, it became clear that Darcey felt a really deep love for her friends. She was beginning to see that the sex they laughed about was not offering the kind of intimate experiences they were hoping for. Instead of wearing her sexual purity as a badge of honour to alienate her from her friends, Darcey began to live out her chastity, and sought to be as supportive and loving to her friends as possible.

I know that her chastity will speak louder to her friends than her words ever could.

Pure power

As well as being free from the need to clock up sexual experience, sexual purity is also about being free from believing the sexual distortions that we see around us in our culture. Sexually pure people are able to see the damaging and empty sexual encounters in novels, films and music for what they really are. They're not fooled by sham romance, or easily persuaded that men who say, 'I love you', and then hit you, are worth sticking with. They are able to understand the impact of what they see and hear, so because they care about their sexuality honouring God, they sometimes switch off, change the topic or walk away.

But as well as all of this, being sexually pure has another dimension that we sometimes overlook, and that's being free from being (or becoming) obsessed about relationships. Sometimes it's really easy to get locked into unhealthy habits, like imagining each worship leader is a potential husband, or thinking you have to rework everything about yourself to be the ultimate girlfriend. Society offers you countless reasons to dislike yourself for being single. There's a never-ending supply of 'perfect' relationships to drool over. By contrast, sexually pure young women know that who they are is who God says that they are, whether they are single, dating, engaged, heartbroken, married, hopeful or despairing. Paul's letter to the Galatians has a lot to say about the freedom we enjoy as Christians: 'Christ has set us free to live a free life. So take your stand! Never again let anyone put a harness of slavery on you' (Galatians 5:1 MSG).

This isn't easy. It requires us to be radical in our lifestyle, to be a sign of God wherever he has placed us. It is shown through:

- the woman who doesn't use social media to elicit sexual approval from other people
- the friends who agree to hold each other accountable for the way they dress, so that they are always presenting the truth about who they are and what they are about

- the couple who agree to protect the unique personal bond that sexual union creates, by setting limits on how, where and when they touch and hold each other
- the woman who is real about her longing for marriage, but chooses to get to know men as friends first so that she doesn't rush into a damaging relationship just to avoid being alone
- the student who listens with nothing but loving compassion to house-mates who have been hurt by casual sex and don't seem able to stop having one-night stands
- the woman struggling with a personal sexual issue who brings it to her loving heavenly Father, knowing that nothing can separate her from his unconditional love.

We lay the foundations for lives of sexual purity when we're not in any relationship. Purity takes practice. Chastity takes courage. And the secret is not to wait until you are in a relationship before you start practising faithfulness.

My husband Jason will never cheat on me.

Now, I know what you're thinking: 'How can she possibly know that?'; 'Maybe he has already done so, but she doesn't know about it!'; 'No-one knows what might happen in the future – if she thinks it could never happen to her, she's deluding herself!'

Of course, that kind of statement provokes all sorts of responses, because absolutely no relationship is perfect. So what I'm about to tell you is not an attempt to put my marriage on a pedestal.

Last week I asked Jason whether he would ever cheat on me. Now, I know it's an odd question, but stick with me for a moment, because what he said got me thinking.

'If I found someone really attractive, I'd run a mile to get away!'

And do you know what? I believe him. Not just because he's my husband, but because I've seen him run – from me!

When we were dating, we wanted to rip each other's clothes off (in private, not public!), but more than that, we wanted to give ourselves fully only to the person we were going to marry. We talked loads about our vision for our sex lives, and agreed that as passionate as we got, we wanted to rein in our sexual exploration until God had made us one. It didn't make dating easier, but it meant that we had some clear boundaries to help us stick to our vision – keep clothed, don't sleep in the same bed and so on.

There were many times when it became really difficult to hold back, and do you know who was the one who walked away to help us stay true to ourselves? Jason. He ran away from situations that would have broken both our hearts in the long run. It was one of the most powerful gifts he gave us as a dating couple – and it made me feel so valued.

I remember during one particularly passionate session, he suddenly got up, grabbed his coat and with a watery smile headed for the door: 'I've got to get out of here, babes.' To his credit, he managed to leave even while I was trying to get him to stay! But as he walked out of the room, I can honestly say that I fell a little deeper in love with him. In that moment I saw his strength, and determined that I would match his courage with mine. From then on, we were both committed to be vigilant for our own chastity.

Going through these experiences together before we even got engaged gives me great confidence that if he needed to do so now, he would run from someone else rather than be unfaithful to me. When he vowed to remain faithful to me 'for as long as we both shall live', he was already practised at faithfulness.

Another nameless girl

One of the main arguments I hear against purity and chastity from young Christians is the fact that in biblical times people would have been married off very young to the cousin of their parents' choice! This may very well be true. Our world would be completely unrecognizable to any of the biblical

characters – just as their world often is to ours. But there's one strange story about chastity that jumps out at me every time I read it.

In the Old Testament, during the dark time of the Judges when God's people were a law unto themselves, there was a stupid father and a chaste daughter.

Jephthah made an oath to God to sacrifice to him the first thing that would come through the door on his return home. (Note that God didn't ask him to make this oath.) You can see what's coming – Jephthah's daughter skips out of the house to greet her father:

> *When he saw her, he tore his clothes in anguish. 'Oh, my daughter!' he cried out. 'You have completely destroyed me! You've brought disaster on me! For I have made a vow to the Lord, and I cannot take it back.'*
>
> *And she said, 'Father, if you have made a vow to the Lord, you must do to me what you have vowed, for the Lord has given you a great victory over your enemies, the Ammonites. But first let me do this one thing: Let me go up and roam in the hills and weep with my friends for two months, because I will die a virgin.'*
>
> *'You may go,' Jephthah said. And he sent her away for two months. She and her friends went into the hills and wept because she would never have children. When she returned home, her father kept the vow he had made, and she died a virgin.*
> (Judges 11:35–39 NLT)

This unsettling story has an air of the macabre about it, but stay with me, because what this nameless girl did next has made sure that her story is heard by every generation who reads the Bible. It also inspired women to start a festival in her honour.

She recognized that within her culture she couldn't go against her father's word (as horrific as it was), so instead, she asked for something else. She asked for time to grieve in the hills with her girlfriends. Her chance of marriage and motherhood, as well as life, had been ripped from her. Yet, rather than going on some crazed bender, chasing all the things that might have been, she chose to embrace who she was, and died a virgin.

There's no way that Jephthah's family is a model of how we should act! I'm also not about to deify his daughter for going to her grave a virgin. It's not a story about virginity; it is, however, a story about what we pursue.

Jephthah was culturally bound to follow through on the promise he made, no matter what, or however barbaric it sounds to us. His daughter was duty-bound to pursue the path to her death. I'm not suggesting that we should copy either of them. But the story challenges me to consider what I see as worth pursuing.

Do I really think that being chaste is worth it?

What do I feel I owe to myself to experience or have before I die?

Can I seriously face the reality that I might choose chastity and never get married?

What if I get married, and then have sex with only my husband for the rest of my life? Am I prepared to pursue chastity if this is what it means?

One path

I often have chats with young unmarried Christian couples who want to enjoy a sexual relationship with the person they love, while still living with integrity as a follower of Jesus. I ask them if they think they can pursue both paths. It's often the case that this is the first time that either of them has thought about what this means. They've not considered what might happen if they break up.

> Premarital sex defrauds the future marriage partner of the person with whom you are involved. You are robbing that person of the virginity and single-minded intimacy that ought to be brought into a marriage. Thus, sexual impurity is as much a social injustice against others as it is a personal sin against God.[14]

Choosing chastity before you are in a relationship, and having these conversations, really helps you get to grips with the issues of handling temptation, recognizing what turns you on and having your own set of boundaries that you are already living within. The boundaries might change a bit when you are in a relationship, but the hard work of thinking about where you would set them, and sticking to them, has already begun.

Acting out a chaste lifestyle before you are in a relationship is one of the best ways to build up the muscles to help you within one. Knowing more about yourself and your responses to sexual stimuli, and practising self-control, are essential if you want to have faithfulness, good communication and realistic expectations in your relationship. God wants you to be sexually pure because he created you to be free and strong. And only a heart fixed on pursuing purity will produce this.

That's why Jason ran. That's why I still choose to run when I'm tempted by other guys, rather than stay and sin.

So if and when you are ready for a relationship, look for the guy who runs like the wind. Who is so determined to love you with all he is and has that he would get up and out of there instead of ever betraying you.

And get fit! There will be times when you will need to run too. You'll be tempted. You'll be drawn into the fantasy of sexual experience without the covenanted commitment God asks of you.

Sexual love is created by God as the expression flowing out of the lasting love that creates the faithful relationships that sexual passion depends on.

This is worth having. It's worth the wait.

It really is.

Wonderland

1. So what have you discovered about yourself, sex and intimacy from any experiences you've had?
2. Do you find yourself sliding rather than deciding when it comes to sex?
3. Do you know the impact that sexualized images, watching sex scenes in films, being in certain situations and so on, have on your values and your confidence in living a sexually pure life?
4. What will you do differently next time to prevent more sexually intimate experiences before marriage?
5. Are you obsessing about being in a relationship, or deceiving yourself that being in the right relationship will make handling sexual temptations easier?
6. Is sexual fidelity in marriage something you seek to be intentional about? If not, what could you do to change this?

My sanctuary

Choosing a life of sexual purity doesn't just happen. The following four steps can be a useful tool to help you orientate yourself around this powerful way of life.

Recognize

To begin with, you need to be honest with yourself about how you're living out your sexual purity. What are you struggling with?

If you're tempted to be too hard on yourself, or not real enough about your struggles, find a friend to reflect with. The goal of sexual purity is to pursue a holy life, whether you're single, dating or married (1 Thessalonians 4:3–5). Holiness simply means a total devotion to God, so ask yourself where your sexual decisions or attitudes are affecting your devotion to God.

Repent

This is your chance to bring your struggles and mistakes to God. If previous sexual experiences or fantasies still have a hold over you, ask Jesus to cut the ties that hold you captive. Clear out any physical or emotional 'memorabilia'. As you learn to repent of the times you sin, you'll discover more and more of God's forgiving and transforming grace and peace.

Restore

Every time we confess to God, he always forgives and restores us. His desire to set you free is always greater than sin's power to destroy you. Which means that when you're forgiven, you know that what's past is behind you, and you get to start over.

Reset

Now it's time to set the boundaries that will free you to live a pure and strong life. Be as detailed and realistic as you can. Ask yourself whether certain behaviours reflect your commitment to honouring your body, your partner and sex as a gift from God for marriage. Clear boundaries will help you to feel more confident in the decisions you make. Think about setting boundaries in the following areas:

1. Entertainment – how can I make sure that the things I choose to watch or listen to don't draw me away from pursuing sexual purity?
2. Body image – how can I dress and behave in ways that enable me to live out my sexual purity?
3. Relationship – where do I need to draw lines around physical and emotional intimacy when I'm dating someone?

It's worth the time, effort and prayer – it really is!

7: BE FAITHFUL

Do you have any idea what's under your bed?

Under my bed is an old box stuffed full of photos of people and places I've loved. I even have scribbled notes from school friends, love letters, my old diary and the odd school report (not sure why!). Sometimes I spend hours trawling through them all, reliving the moments the images conjure up. My favourite is an old black-and-white photo of my granny who died years ago. She's sitting at her table gazing out of the window, oblivious of the fact that she's being photographed, captivated by something far away – at the end of the garden maybe? Or by a memory that lies deep within her? She's perfectly still as she's yielded to the moment that's holding her, heart and soul.

Sometimes we think that our life as followers of Jesus should look like this. Sorted. Focused. Confident. If anyone were to ask us what we're doing with our life, we'd be able to reel off a list of things we know that God has called

us to do. We'd know all the big stuff, like what job we'll do, who we're going to marry, what we're going to call our pet lizard (Nebuchadnezzar, by the way). Our eyes are fixed firmly on the prize, and nothing will distract us from our goal!

But the reality is quite different.

There's another photo in my box that I always look for. It's of me and some school friends on a trip to France. We're a huddle of smiling girls with long fluffy hair and matching backpacks. But none of the clothes I'm wearing are mine. It's a photo that reminds me of how it felt to be confused, uncomfortable in my friend's clothes, and sixteen! I had no idea how my life would pan out. I wanted to live for Jesus. Be all sold out for him. But I had no idea really what that would look like.

I just wanted God to tell me what to do.

Desperately.

If you were to flick through the pages of my teenage diary, you'd see time and time again my frantic scribbles: 'Please God, tell me what to do! I want my life to matter. Show me the way!'

Does this ring any bells for you?

But as well as our hunger to please God, our longing to know what he thinks we should do is sometimes about avoiding risk. There's always a risk factor to the big decisions we make in life. What will happen if I 'settle' on this university course, this marriage partner, this career? So we shouldn't be too hard on ourselves for wanting to be certain that things are going to work out well.

But wanting someone else to make the decision for us can also be another kind of cushion: it means we've got someone to blame if it all goes wrong. Sometimes, by looking for the 'sign' that something is God's will, we're really wanting someone else to take responsibility. I often chat with young women who feel crippled with indecision about their life choices. They're so eager not to let God and their family or friends down, that they almost resort to being a little kid again and expecting everyone else, including God, to make their decisions for them. Or they surge ahead into a course of action, relationship or new job, convinced that God must be 'in it' as doors have opened so easily, only to do a complete U-turn the following week when problems arise.

Kim had been praying for the right opportunity to move out of home for so long. Eventually, she found a perfect little flat just round the corner from her new job. Her parents seemed pleased too, and helped to pay the rent for the first two months as she settled in. Finally, she felt the freedom she had been craving, but then she wobbled. One Sunday after the service, she came and found me where I was hanging out in the crèche.

'I don't think God did want me to move out of home after all. Do you think he did, or did I just get that one wrong?'

'What makes you think that you heard wrongly?' I asked. 'You seemed so sure last week that it was the right decision to make.'

'It's just been little things,' she explained, 'but they've got me a bit stressed. Like the boiler has broken down in the flat, and the neighbours are being so difficult about where I can leave my bicycle.'

In many ways, she really wanted to know, 'God, if this is your plan for me, then why isn't it easier?'

Moving out of home to be nearer her first ever job was probably one of the most significant and solo decisions Kim had ever made, so it was understand-able that she sought approval for her decision. Like many of us, she grew up with a number of people speaking into her life and telling her their version of what she should do. She'd heard so many talks about God having good plans for her life, but coupled with the pressure she felt to get it right, the sinking feeling that she might have got it wrong was proving too much.

Wouldn't life be simpler if God just told us clearly what he wanted us to do?

Simpler yes, but not better.

Life isn't simple. So, when things prove to be more difficult than we had hoped, that isn't a sign that we misheard God. It's a sign that we're living. So I've got some advice for you. Don't wait around in your favourite coffee shop for divine intervention to map out your life's course – it won't happen! Why? Because God is more interested in your growth than your comfort. He wants your love for him to grow, so that over time you not only have a stronger sense of what he might want you to do, but a greater willingness to do it.

Clingy

There's a wonderful story of a young trainee Jesuit priest who spent three months in the slums of Calcutta with Mother Teresa before he took his final vows. As he worked tirelessly in the 'House of Dying', John Kavanaugh wrestled with whether or not he should return to his life in America, or give himself completely to the poor of India. One day he asked Mother Teresa to pray that God would give him clarity about what he should do with his life. She apparently refused his request. When he asked her why, she is recorded as having said, 'Clarity is the last thing you are clinging to, and must let go of. I have never had clarity; what I have always had is trust. So I will pray that you trust God.'[15]

Whenever people tell their stories of God calling them, they tend to head for the highlights, like the word they received from someone at the end of a meeting. But if we were to look at their lives as a whole, we'd see a very different story. For all the one-off God moments of sheer clarity, there would be weeks, months, even years, of silence and sacrifice. Where all they knew to do was to choose to live for Jesus in every ordinary moment.

I have a friend who's a well-known and loved worship leader. Whenever she's at events, people queue up round the block to ask her how they can get to where she is. It always makes her laugh, because the place 'she is' most of the time is living her regular life for the audience of One in her local church, at home with her family or out with friends who don't know how amazing Jesus is. In the scheme of her whole life, her platform moments are precious and few.

Often the people we see up on platforms or in places of influence and calling have had tough journeys getting there. Being significant wasn't their first thought. Being surrendered was. Before they felt the calling of God, they knew the sacrifice that came with living for God. Of being broken and rebuilt in his image. They had no idea what God was going to do with their lives; they only knew they could choose whether to trust him or not. And as they did, they began to catch the heartbeat of a God who is always looking for people to join him in reaching the lost, the last and the least. Serving his great mission would mean nothing less than complete trust, total surrender. But it would also ensure an experience of life that would be amazingly full: 'This is what my Father wants: that anyone who sees the Son and trusts who he is and what he does and then aligns with him will enter *real* life, *eternal* life' (John 6:40 MSG).

Such life will spill out and touch others.

There is one aspect of our calling that we can be really clear about: it will involve us suffering in some way. This is not the kind of message we always hear in churches or from other Christians. I know that as a speaker at events, I sometimes shy away from this truth because I don't want to come across too 'heavy'. But God opened my eyes to how ludicrous my thinking was a few years ago at a festival where I was speaking.

It had been raining solidly for days, so the mud in the marquee was almost knee-high in places. As I started my talk, rolls of thunder shook the tent so hard that the power supply cut out. I had to shout as I tried to stay in view of the car headlights that were beaming onto the stage. It was crazy! To top it all, I was still determined to do the elaborate prayer-station-type response, with the softly spoken prayer and plinky-plonky music I had planned. But it became increasingly obvious that no-one in their right mind was going to get out of their seat and do anything except go home!

I finished, stepped off the stage and sank to my knees in the mud. The tools I normally took to the stage with me (cool images, film clips, nifty responses) had been stripped away, and all that was left was an insecure woman, hungry for God, but doubting what he had called her to do. I knelt there for what felt like ages as the tent doors flapped in the howling wind.

Then I saw something that took my breath away.

As I got up to move, I was surrounded by young people kneeling in the mud too. They were filthy and they were hungry for God. They knew that life was hard, and that following Jesus makes life even more complicated. They knew that no-one gets richer or escapes suffering by following Jesus. Kneeling in the mud with these incredible disciples has stayed with me as one of the most real and raw responses to God's Word that I have ever experienced. I have no doubt that some of them have gone on to suffer in different ways for their love of Jesus. My hope is that each one is still growing in their trust of God and their willingness to keep kneeling in the mud and surrender all that they are for his sake.

That night God showed me that he is in the business of calling. We are to be in the business of surrendering.

Even Jesus, who lived the most significant life of any human being, knew that the sacrifice is the calling. So, as he drew near to Jerusalem and his death, he ramped up his teaching on suffering. If his disciples had missed the fact that following him meant walking the path of pain, they were now about to get it loud and clear.

Then he said to them all: 'Whoever wants to be my disciple must deny themselves and take up their cross daily and follow me. For whoever

wants to save their life will lose it, but whoever loses their life for me will save it. What good is it for someone to gain the whole world, and yet lose or forfeit their very self?
(Luke 9:23–25 NIV)

Following Jesus is not about becoming a better person, but becoming a new person. But our transformation doesn't stop at the point where we say yes to Jesus. In fact, it starts there. Every day we need to say yes to the new creation God is shaping us into. That's what it means to yield yourself to God. It's the daily and deliberate handing over of your will to God. And it can hurt sometimes, because we're rebels by inclination.

Can you see what God wants you to do with your life?

Surrender it.

Solid

Only one woman's story in the Bible starts with 'Once upon a time . . .' (*The Message* translation), and true to form, it has a very happy ending. Ruth's is a life poured out in love for her grieving and broken widowed mother-in-law Naomi. Eventually, she gets the guy (Boaz), and joins the dynasty that will stretch all the way to Jesus himself! But Ruth didn't know about any of this when she chose to stay and to love.

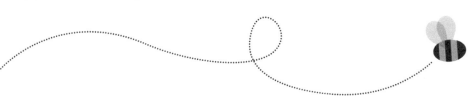

Her story begins with her marriage to an Israelite man, and then follow ten uneventful years in her new family's home. But tragedy strikes, and in quick succession her husband, father-in-law and brother-in-law all die. Marooned in Moab at a time of great famine, this trio of grieving women had the choice to stay and maybe die from starvation, or head their own separate ways to find food and a future for themselves. Mother-in-law Naomi urges both women to go back home. Orpah leaves, but Ruth goes with Naomi.

> *But Ruth said, 'Don't force me to leave you; don't make me go home. Where you go, I go; and where you live, I'll live. Your people are my people, your God is my god; where you die, I'll die, and that's where I'll be buried, so help me God – not even death itself is going to come between us!'*
> (Ruth 1:16–17 MSG)

Ruth's loyalty goes beyond what would have been expected for a woman of her time. She's paid her dues, so she's free to head home to make something of the rest of her life. Instead, she surrenders her future for the love of a broken woman. We're not told if she agonized over her decision to put Naomi's well-being first, but I get the feeling that in that moment it was crystal clear what she should do. Surrender. Later, she is one of the four women named as Jesus' ancestors. But she started by sacrificing everything when she had no certainty of any reward or recognition.

Like many of the women in the Bible whose stories have inspired me, her actions go further than simple compliance within her culture. There's something about her response to Naomi that thunders down the generations to us as the voice of a woman who chooses to be available to God.

If anyone is a poster girl for selfless surrender, it's Ruth.

Instinct

If we're to be poster girls for anything, surely it's this. That the only life worth having is the one that's spent in the service of God. The older I get, the less interested I am in any other kind of life. You can spend your days chasing a whole bunch of things that might get you money in the bank and letters after your name (not bad things in themselves), but at some point or other, Jesus will ask you whether you'd be willing to abandon everything for him.

Our lives are meant to be a stark contrast to the emptiness of life without surrender to Christ.

For Paul, surrender to Christ was not only what we're destined for, but the only way to live. As he trod this path, he discovered something that our brothers and sisters around the globe who suffer for knowing Christ have also discovered. That nothing life can offer, including life itself, can compare to knowing Jesus.

Listening to Paul speaking about his eagerness to lay it all down for Jesus almost makes it sound like surrender came easy to him. Yet he was regularly tortured and imprisoned for not shutting up about Christ. It wouldn't have been easy, but maybe it became instinctive, like breathing. Maybe his deepening relationship with Jesus meant that over time what he needed to do became as clear as day.

When I stop to think about the number of people sharing planet earth with me who don't know that all their pain, suffering and hopelessness can be met and matched with a love and hope that will rock their world, I feel a tightening in my chest. It makes me focus on asking myself some questions that I won't like the sound of, never mind the answers!

- When did I last reach out to someone whom I find challenging?
- Why do I spend so much time and energy trying to be liked by important people, when Jesus is asking me to lay it all down for the lost, the last and the least?
- What's stopping me in this moment from choosing the tough path of surrender to Jesus? Fear of rejection or of looking stupid? My greed in wanting to keep my things for myself? My ambition to make myself more well known than Jesus?

Be faithful

I am continually humbled by the thought that one day I will get to spend eternity with sisters and brothers who gave their everything, even their lives, rather than deny the One who gave it all for them. Find ways to keep them in your mind and heart as you grow in your own discipleship journey.

Listen to Paul:

> *Yes, all the things I once thought were so important are gone from my life. Compared to the high privilege of knowing Christ Jesus as my Master, firsthand, everything I once thought I had going for me is insignificant . . . I've dumped it all in the trash so I could embrace Christ and be embraced by him.*
> (Philippians 3:8–9 MSG)

I think I need to know what tomorrow holds. But I don't. What I need is to know the One who holds all my tomorrows. Then I need to trust him enough to give it all to him and for him. Even if it means losing in this life. This is the secret to experiencing life in all its fullness. It doesn't get any better than this.

But I wouldn't give my life for anything less – would you?

Wonderland

Denying ourselves doesn't mean ignoring the way God has made us, and how he might want to use it all for his glory. Exploring who we are is a powerful way to bring ourselves fully to God for his service.

The evangelist J.John often uses a really helpful illustration to help kick-start this process of self-awareness that can lead us towards surrendering ourselves to God:

S = spiritual gifts. Read the whole of 1 Corinthians 12 and identify the gifts God is giving you. They are all expressions of God's power, and so they aren't presents to stay on a shelf, but tools to be used to serve God's body and his mission.

H = heart. Jesus said that whatever we do for the least, we do for him. When you think of the least, who comes to mind? Who is on your heart to reach out to with God's love?

A = abilities. You possess the ability to do all sorts of things, some of them really well. God is a huge fan of your intelligence and skills. He created you uniquely, and can speak to you and others through these abilities. So what are they?

P = personality. There is a unique combination of characteristics and qualities that make up your personality. You won't always be aware of them, so you might need to ask friends and family to name them.

E = experiences. You have seen and felt things that have left an impression on your life. Both positive and negative, these have given you insight into the lives of people that others might not have.

When we talk about surrendering ourselves for the sake of the gospel, we mean that we give our SHAPE for God to use as he will. He takes what we offer, and uses it all to bring his peace and wholeness to others. Are you quick to sense injustice? God is asking you to challenge those situations and institutions where people are treated wrongly or unfairly. Are you a fine-detail person? Do you handle money well? God is asking you to help someone break out of the cycle of debt and despair.

When you see your whole self as an offering to God, you begin to see your life and future in different ways. Instead of asking, 'Does God want me to go to university?', the question becomes: 'How will going to university help me grow in my relationship with Jesus and my opportunity to serve him?' Instead of asking, 'Does God want me to date anyone?', the question becomes: 'How will dating deepen my love of God and my willingness to serve him through all my relationships?'

And so, dear brothers and sisters, I plead with you to give your bodies to God because of all he has done for you. Let them be a living and holy sacrifice – the kind he will find acceptable. This is truly the way to worship him. Don't copy the behaviour and customs of this world, but let God

transform you into a new person by changing the way you think. Then you will learn to know God's will for you, which is good and pleasing and perfect.
(Romans 12:1–3 NLT)

My sanctuary

Lots of us feel anxiety about an uncertain future. We don't know what's around the corner, and more often than not, God doesn't tell us. When Mother Teresa prayed for trust rather than clarity for the young priest, she wasn't denying his desire to know what he should do. But she was responding to his deeper desire to know that he was safe and secure in God's hands, whatever he did. Hundreds of years before this, a nun called Julian of Norwich (1342–1413) referred to such trust as an 'enfolding'.

We are enfolded in the Father, and we are enfolded in the Son and we are enfolded in the Holy Spirit. The Father is enfolded in us, and the Son is enfolded in us, and the Holy Spirit is enfolded in us; All-mighty, All-wisdom, All-goodness: one God, one Lord.[16]

Close your eyes, and ask God to show you how he is folding you into himself. You're tucked in. Held. Secure. Safe. So yield it all to him, and watch what he does.

8: BE LOVE

Years ago I met Cleo.

I was working in a hostel for young homeless people. Cleo was there because, after years of emotional abuse, she had finally decided to run away from home. Unsurprisingly, she had developed a tough persona to cope with the brutality she had experienced. One night she took a toxic combination of prescription pills and vodka. After she got back from hospital, she spent every day locked in her room, crying, angry, hurting – with a pulse, but without a life.

One afternoon my manager asked me to take Cleo out for some fresh air. It was a beautiful day. We got into my cranky Nova car and drove up a very steep hill to a place of outstanding natural beauty in East Sussex called Beachy Head. When you stand at the top of the cliff, you literally feel like you're on top of the world, with nothing but sea and sky stretching out before

you. It's a place of infinite possibilities. It's also the place where people come from miles around to jump to their deaths. Even now I'm not sure why I got it into my head to bring a girl who had tried to take her life to a cliff infamous for suicide.

But I did.

After a while we got out of the car and began to walk to the edge of the cliff. We stood in the warm sea breeze. Cleo spoke first: 'I'm dead inside. I'm not really living.'

'What could change that?' I asked.

'Who knows?' came the reply.

We stood in silence a bit more. Then I whispered, 'I'm alive.'

The seagulls screeched below us, and in the distance you could hear the tractors working the fields, churning up the rich earth. Life was all around us.

'I'm alive,' I said a little louder. 'Hey! I'm alive! Look at me! I'm alive!' I jumped up. 'Come on, I'm alive! This is my life!' I was shouting now, and waving my arms about.

Cleo watched me and began to giggle.

'You're an idiot,' she said.

'I know, and I don't care!' I shouted back. 'We're alive, Cleo. Here, today, now, in this moment! Alive! Shout it out! Tell the birds and the sky and the sea. Shout it out to the hospital. Let them hear it. Shout it to your past, to your family. Let them hear you. Let me hear you. Let yourself hear you. You're alive, Cleo! You're alive!'

Eventually we were both hopping around and shouting, 'I'm alive!' at the tops of our voices. I'm sure we scared away a bus load of grey-haired tourists, but we didn't care. We were grabbing at the life that Cleo had nearly given up on. It felt like nothing we'd ever known. I knew that the life-bringing Spirit of Jesus was dancing with us on that cliff edge that day. He was the one who was offering Cleo the irresistible invitation to live. To know love on the other side of pain. I know he has never stopped chasing Cleo as she's attempted to rebuild her life out of the ashes of her near death.

All the best stories are about life conquering death.

They're about the tables being turned, the underdog coming out on top, love winning the day. This is your story: your life has been rescued and your eyes have been opened by Love. You are loved over and over again, in countless ways, by the God who never changes and whose promises are new every morning. We have complete access to a love that nothing can destroy.

> *Love is as strong as death,*
> *its jealousy as enduring as the grave.*
> *Love flashes like fire,*
> *the brightest kind of flame.*
> *Many waters cannot quench love,*
> *nor can rivers drown it.*
> (Song of Solomon 8:6–7 NLT)

Shout it out . . .

'I'm loved! I'm his beloved! Nothing can wrench me out of God's heart. I'm loved for good. I'm loved forever!'

Being loved like this means something life changing. Our divine rescue from sin doesn't simply mean we're warehoused for heaven once we die. It's an irresistible invitation to live a life of love here on earth. To live out our one, wild, rescued and beloved life for the glory of the One who first loved us.

We're called to be love.

This book has featured some of the heroines I adore. Beautiful women I've met in the pages of the Bible and in my everyday life who challenge me to break free from pressures to be less than I am. The way they reach out to God and others in love, even when they doubt their worth and ability, inspires me to dare to believe that I could be as daring, as loving.

In the book of Joshua we meet Rahab.

We know little about her, other than her profession as a prostitute in the highly fortified city of Jericho. I'm not sure that we're supposed to try to be like her. She's not a classic role model for a Christian woman! But she's fearless in her act of resistance, and she has faith, and that's why we know about her.

Rahab's story is tucked away in the pages of the Old Testament at a time of huge significance for God's people. They'd been rescued some forty years before from the inhumane slavery of Egypt, and had finally reached the dreamland God had promised them so long ago: Canaan. But there were still some battles ahead of them, one of which was to destroy the powerfully fortified city of Jericho.

They succeed. It's a bloody chapter in Israel's history; the Bible tells us that no-one in Jericho survived. No-one, that is, except Rahab and her family. They survived because her act of treason against her own people in hiding the Israelite spies ensured that the people of God got the info they needed to launch a devastating attack on Jericho.

What made Rahab risk life and limb for people she didn't even know? How is this in any way a story of love?

For starters, it's not really Rahab's story.

It's not her victory. It's not her courage that won the day, or the position of her house on the walls of the city. It's not her ability to glean information from strangers, propelling her towards a shift in loyalties, or even about her growing love for a nomadic group of people.

This is God's story. His victory. His power. His love.

It always is.

What did Rahab make of this God who fights for his own? A God whose love for his people knows no bounds. Who parts the waves and drowns their enemies, feeds them with a miracle food every morning and gently leads them by fire and cloud. Did her heart begin to melt towards the God who demonstrated a fierce love she had never known?

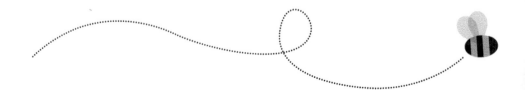

*I know that the L*ORD *has given this land to you and that a great fear of you has fallen on us, so that all who live in this country are melting in fear because of you. We have heard how the L*ORD *dried up the water of the Red Sea for you when you came out of Egypt, and what you did to Sihon and Og, the two kings of the Amorites east of the Jordan, whom you completely destroyed. When we heard of it, our hearts sank and everyone's courage failed because of you, for the L*ORD *your God is God in heaven above and on the earth below.*
(Joshua 2:9–11 NIV)

God loves with a mighty love, and he invites us to love in exactly the same way that he loves.

Fast forward to the New Testament, and Jesus preaches a radical message of love. Love the unlovely, the difficult to love, the stranger, the family member who pushes you away. Don't love just when it's easy. Love because everything in you wants to hate, hold back or hide away from this person. Love when the very act of reaching out opens you up to all kinds of rejection and ridicule. We might think that this kind of love is only about boarding a plane to the latest war zone, or giving away everything you have that you don't need.

Don't let anything stop you from loving like that. Give it all away at least once.

But you and I know that being loving to people we meet in our everyday life can be just as challenging. Who are your enemies? Who do you just simply not like? Who do you not defend when others backchat about them? Who are you happy to see leave the room?

Those names that popped into your mind are your opportunity to live differently. Here's your chance to live out the truth that, as you are loved so completely, you have nothing to lose in loving others. In fact, you have it all to gain!

> *I tell you, love your enemies. Help and give without expecting a return. You'll never – I promise – regret it. Live out this God-created identity the way our Father lives toward us, generously and graciously, even when we're at our worst. Our Father is kind; you be kind.*
> (Luke 6:35–36 MSG)

I imagine that sometimes you're impulsive, passionate, unpredictable. I reckon that, like me, you have a tendency at times to be selfish, rebellious, doubting. There are times when you love yourself and times when you doubt yourself. But you're loved so passionately and completely that you can find your feet and learn to live from a heart that's been melted and made whole by a Saviour who will love you now and into eternity.

This is your life; you're breathtaking. And you're called to pour yourself out in love, as love. Day after day after day.

God has not only rescued you; he's changing you and drawing you into a deeper, more reckless love than you've ever known. Your life is no longer your own. It's a wonderful offering of worship to the One who calls you to love as you've been loved. For people to know that you belong to him because of the love that radiates from you.

> *Let me give you a new command: Love one another. In the same way I loved you, you love one another. This is how everyone will recognize that you are my disciples – when they see the love you have for each other.*
> (John 13:34–35 MSG)

It won't be easy.

You've got some mountains ahead of you that your love for Jesus will compel you to climb. You'll reveal your beauty where there's only the ugliness of lies and pain; you'll love selflessly, even when others have given up; you'll fight injustices, even when people try to silence you.

Where is God asking you to be love? Where's the 'here' he's asking you to call home? Where will you bear the fruit of a life surrendered to him? City, slum, countryside, desert, housing estate? Your life will be extraordinary because you'll heal the sick here in Jesus' name. You'll get a job here. Cast out demons here. You'll raise children here. Pay your taxes here. Feed the hungry here. You'll vote or even stand in local elections here. Care for the environment here. You'll be a generous leader and a humble servant here. You'll learn to love people more, and you'll learn to love yourself more here. You'll be disappointed and anointed. You'll be beautiful and broken and brilliant.

What I'm discovering is that I only do anything lasting when I do it for the sake of Love. When I step out of the safety of the boat onto the crashing waves. When I realize that beneath my feet might be water, but with me is the One who is greater than the storm.

There is nothing like Love.

He is already eternally yours,

And his love will always find you.

So be full of love, be free in love and be fierce in being love, as you grow in knowing that you are God's beloved.

Rachel x

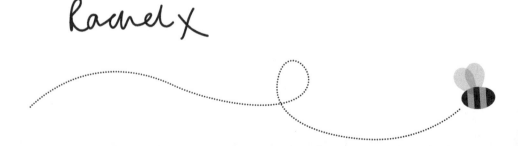

To me – Jesus is my God.

Jesus is my Spouse.

Jesus is my Life.

Jesus is my only Love.

Jesus is my All in all.

Jesus is my everything.

Jesus, I love with my whole heart, with my whole being.

I have given Him all, even my sins, and He has espoused me to Himself in all tenderness and love.[17]

NOTES

1. Rend Collective, 'True Intimacy', from the album, *Homemade Worship by Handmade People* (2011).
2. I remember once hearing a journalist referring to Beyoncé as a 'fierce woman'. The word 'fierce' has recently been adopted by our culture to mean 'confident' and 'determined'. We're not Beyoncé, and our lives are not lived out on a stage in front of adoring fans. We live for an audience of One: God. So our confidence comes from our identity as beloved women, and our determination comes from our hunger to see people transformed by God's love and his Word.
3. Bill Johnson, *Hosting the Presence: Unveiling Heaven's Agenda* (Destiny Image, 2013), p. 131.
4. John Ortberg, www.goodreads.com/quotes/522172-god-sees-with-utter-clarity-who-we-are-he-is (accessed 20 April 2015).

5. Kenneth E. Bailey, *Jesus Through Middle Eastern Eyes: Cultural Studies in the Gospels* (SPCK, 2008), pp. 189–275.

6. See Kat Cannon, 'Designed to Be Brave', www.todayschristianwoman. com/articles/2013/september/designed-to-be-brave.html (accessed 13 April 2015).

7. Lisa Hickey, 'Chasing Beauty: An Addict's Memoir', http:// goodmenproject.com/featured-content/chasing-beauty-and-addicts-memoir (accessed 20 April 2015).

8. From a talk given by John O'Donohue at Greenbelt 2004: 'Divine Beauty: The Invisible Embrace', www.greenbelt.org.uk/media/ talks/13985-john-odonohue.

9. From her 'Essence' speech. See http://www.vulture.com/2014/02/ read-lupita-nyongs-moving-essence-speech.html (accessed 25 March 2015).

10. Steve Maraboli, see www.goodreads.com/work/quotes/14708444-life-the-truth-and-being-free (accessed 20 April 2015).

11. Rachel Gardner and André Adefope, *The Dating Dilema: A Romance Revolution* (Inter-Varsity Press, 2013), p. 137.

12. Judith K. Balswick and Jack O. Balswick, *Authentic Human Sexuality: An Integrated Christian Approach* (IVP Academic, 2008), p. 69.

13. Dietrich Bonhoeffer, *Letters and Papers from Prison*, abridged edn (SCM, 1971), p. 141.

14. Sam Storms: read more at http://www.whatchristianswanttoknow. com/20-christian-quotes-about-purity/#ixzz3TAgi3MiT.

15. Cited in Paula Rinehart, *Strong Women, Soft Hearts: A Woman's Guide to Cultivating a Wise Heart and a Passionate Life* (Thomas Nelson, 2005), p. 82.
16. Cited in *Pocket Prayers*, compiled by Christopher Herbert (Church House, 2004), p. 8.
17. Mother Teresa, cited in Cris Rogers, *Immeasurably More* (Lion Hudson, 2015), p. 99.

also by Rachel Gardner

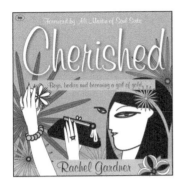

Cherished
Boys, bodies and becoming a girl of gold
Rachel Gardner

ISBN: 978-1-84474-389-6
160 pages, paperback

In this gutsy and intimate book, Rachel Gardner tackles head-on the issues facing teenage girls: self-image, the pull of the in-crowd, puberty, boys, sex, regrets and godly ambition. *Cherished* is credible, yet shot through with biblical wisdom, and parents and youthworkers can give this book with confidence.

To her readers, she writes, 'I have written this book for you. I realize that you don't know me, so it might feel a bit weird me saying that. But it's true. I have written this book because I want to let you in on a bit of a secret: you are precious and your life is a gift to you. It's a secret because few of us know it and fewer actually believe it. I hope you will feel inspired to explore your abilities and dreams, be encouraged to protect your heart and still keep it open to God and others, appreciate your life and the mysteries in the world around you. May these words of wisdom help you know that you are lovely, lovable, unique, full of potential and, above all, cherished.' Rachel x

Available from your local Christian bookshop or **www.thinkivp.com**

also by Rachel Gardner

The Dating Dilemma
A romance revolution
Rachel Gardner & André Adefope

ISBN: 978-1-84474-623-1
192 pages, paperback

Boy meets girl. Boy and girl go on romantic dates. Boy and girl establish healthy boundaries, share their hearts and fall in love. Boy buys ring. Girl says, 'yes'. Boy and girl get married ... If only it was this simple!

How do you recognize real love amidst the multitude of other things that go hand in hand with it: infatuation, lust, desperation, attraction, hate? How do you know if the person you are going out with is the person you should spend the rest of your life with? How easy is it to get it wrong?'

Rachel Gardner and André Adefope look at God's guidelines for romance. They ask the difficult questions, but they also ask how God helps us to change – how you can become a godly boyfriend: confident in who you are, supportive, worthy of respect; or a godly girlfriend: sure of yourself, able to nurture selflessness and generosity in relationships.

Available from your local Christian bookshop or **www.thinkivp.com**

Inter-Varsity Press

For more information about IVP and our
publications visit **www.ivpbooks.com**

Get regular updates at **ivpbooks.com/signup**
Find us on **facebook.com/ivpbooks**
Follow us on **twitter.com/ivpbookcentre**

Inter-Varsity Press, a company limited by guarantee registered in England and Wales, number 05202650. Registered
office IVP Bookcentre, Norton Street, Nottingham NG7 3HR, United Kingdom. Registered charity number 1105757.